A VERY SHORT,
FAIRLY INTERESTING AND
REASONABLY CHEAP BOOK ABOUT

GLOBALIZATION

A VERY SHORT, FAIRLY INTERESTING AND REASONABLY CHEAP BOOK ABOUT

GLOBALIZATION

LEO McCANN

Los Angeles | London | New Delhi
Singapore | Washington DC | Melbourne

Los Angeles | London | New Delhi
Singapore | Washington DC | Melbourne

SAGE Publications Ltd
1 Oliver's Yard
55 City Road
London EC1Y 1SP

SAGE Publications Inc.
2455 Teller Road
Thousand Oaks, California 91320

SAGE Publications India Pvt Ltd
B 1/I 1 Mohan Cooperative Industrial Area
Mathura Road
New Delhi 110 044

SAGE Publications Asia-Pacific Pte Ltd
3 Church Street
#10-04 Samsung Hub
Singapore 049483

Editor: Matthew Waters
Senior assistant editor: Jasleen Kaur
Production editor: Sarah Cooke
Copyeditor: Christine Bitten
Proofreader: Fabienne Pedroletti
Indexer: Martin Hargreaves
Marketing manager: Alison Borg
Cover design: Wendy Scott
Typeset by C&M Digitals (P) Ltd, Chennai, India
Printed in the UK

The title for the 'A Very Short, Fairly Interesting and Reasonably Cheap Book about...Series' was devised by Chris Grey. His book, *A Very Short, Fairly Interesting and Reasonably Cheap Book about Studying Organizations*, was the founding title of this series. Chris Grey asserts his right to be recognized as founding editor of the A Very Short, Fairly Interesting and Reasonably Cheap Book about... Series.

Library of Congress Control Number: 2017948736

British Library Cataloguing in Publication data

A catalogue record for this book is available from the British Library

ISBN 978-1-47391-910-5
ISBN 978-1-47391-911-2 (pbk)

Contents

About the Author

Leo McCann is Professor of Organisation Studies at Alliance Manchester Business School, the University of Manchester. His research focuses on globalization, political economy and critical studies of management, work and organization. He is especially interested in how the 'global' forces of economic change impact on workplaces and occupations, especially white-collar, professional organizations. Workplaces and occupational settings where Leo has conducted qualitative and ethnographic research include those of corporate middle management (banks, automotive manufacturers, insurance companies), as well as public service professions (emergency services, healthcare and the military). He is currently working on a new book on England's ambulance services and the paramedic profession. Leo's work has been published in journals such as *Human Relations, Journal of Management Studies, Organization, Public Administration,* and *Human Resource Management,* and he is currently one of the editors-in-chief of *Competition & Change* (a journal of globalization, political economy and financialization). His books include *Capitalism and Business* (Sage, 2015), *International and Comparative Business* (Sage, 2014), *Managing in the Modern Corporation* (Cambridge University Press, 2009) and *Deconstructing the Welfare State* (Routledge, 2015). He teaches courses on globalization, US society, professional work and ethnographic research methods.

Acknowledgements

I want to thank several people who have influenced how this book came together. Firstly, it was Matthew Waters at Sage who approached me with the ominous prospect of writing a 'Very Short' book on this trifling matter of 'Globalization'. A chance meeting with Philip Wake of the Spirit of Football Community Interest Charity helped me to decide to take on Matthew's challenge. It was Philip who introduced me to the ex-globalization academic David Goldblatt's brilliant writings on football. Our random discussion on that train journey to London ranged over football, business, and the outer layers of Shakira's management team. That was all I needed to convince me I had to write this book. Matthew was a fantastic editor to work with – several of the points and examples discussed in this volume are direct responses to his creative, helpful promptings. I'd also like to thank the undergraduate students who took my 'Global Contexts of Business and Management' course at Manchester. I hope that students enjoy this text and I'm always happy to share ideas; if readers have any comments about the book that they'd like to share, please feel free to contact me via Twitter on: @LeoMc76

Many ideas and concepts expressed here emerged from regular discussions with fellow academics and PhD students associated in some way with the E floor of the MBS East building at the University of Manchester. These include Charlotte Coleman, Ian Crowther, Julie Froud, Ed Granter, John Hassard, Damian Hodgson, Debra Howcroft, Paula Hyde, Wojciek Kwiatkowski, Gemma Lord, Miguel Martinez Lucio, Stephen Mustchin, Damian O'Doherty, Dean Pierides, Daniel Tischer, Brian Wierman and Karel Williams. Whatever globalization throws at us, we will always have our E floor. (Or should it be our E-Ring?) My sincere thanks to all of you.

Introduction

Globalization at Christmas, on the High Seas and in Outer Space

For much of the world – perhaps for around a third of the global population that describes itself as Christian – the 25th of December is Christmas Day. One of the most important dates of the Christian calendar, it marks the birth of Jesus; in Christian doctrine, the son of God and redeemer of mankind's sins. The date shares ancient symbolic resonance, coinciding with Roman rituals such as Saturnalia and the Pagan Winter Solstice from which the traditions of gift-giving and Yule logs might derive. In today's hyperglobalized Western world, Christmas is one of the few moments in the calendar year that can provide reflection and release from the incessant pace of life that characterizes today's supercharged capitalism.

But Christmas is far from immune to the imperatives of global capitalism. It has long been common to bemoan the commercializing of Christmas and its exhausting excess of shopping, cooking and consuming. Christmas, since at least Victorian times, has been a commercial project (Hancock and Rehn, 2011) and today has mushroomed into an orgy of borrowing, spending and consuming – a form of intensified seasonal project work from which one has to recover with a New Year's healthy living drive. December brings 'Black Fridays' of hard discounting in which overzealous shoppers are seen crushed in supermarket doorways or fighting over tripled-sized plasma screens. Police, ambulance services and hospital staff struggle to deal with a Yuletide swelling of drunk and injured revelers, especially the overspill from office parties all held on the same Friday before Christmas. Rampant consumerism seems to have hijacked a supposedly sacred season.

And yet it could still be said that Christmases in global consumer capitalism retain a sense of magic and epiphany. They even feature visitations from far-off lands. Take a container ship inbound from China as an example. These miraculous beasts seem to defy the laws of physics. The largest vessels weigh around 50,000 tonnes unloaded, can carry nearly 20,000 containers and over a 100,000 tonnes of cargo. The design and construction trends are for ever-larger vessels, requiring governments to extend and redesign canals and ports to service them.

They find their way across thousands of miles of ocean by following a celestial network of high-technology navigation satellites such as the USA's GPS, Russia's GLONASS, or the EU's Galileo system. Goods from afar will stock Western shops in time for the holiday period, for which some workers have been paid a Christmas bonus and many retailers will hope to achieve as much as half of their full year's volume of sales (Bozkurt, 2015: 479). Philosopher Alain de Botton in *The Pleasures and Sorrows of Work* here describes one of these giant hulks homing into view at London's Tilbury docks:

> The ship's course alone is impressive. Three weeks earlier she set off from Yokohama and since then she has called in at Yokkaichi, Shenzen, Mumbai, Istanbul, Casablanca and Rotterdam. Only days before, as dull rain fell on the sheds of Tilbury, she began her ascent up the Red Sea under a relentless sun, circled by a family of storks from Djibouti. The steel cranes now moving over her hull break up a miscellaneous cargo of fan ovens, running shoes, calculators, fluorescent bulbs, cashew nuts and vividly coloured toy animals. Her boxes of Moroccan lemons will end up on the shelves of central London shops by evening. There will be new television sets in York at dawn. (de Botton, 2009: 15)

De Botton, in a typically elegant paragraph, introduces us to the complexities and interconnectedness of global capitalism, making the strange familiar and the familiar strange. While this passage largely celebrates the exoticism and distance-destroying nature of globalization, a reader can detect a hint of critique at the oddness and irrationality of toy animals from China and lemons from Morocco. Why have we come to expect television sets at dawn?

One reading of our increasingly globalized economy marvels at the extent, diversity, complexity and newness of global trade; in the shipping example above this includes the international logistics, the multinational crew of the vessels, the powerful computing and engineering systems that keep the global economy afloat and enable the 24/7 availability of the bountiful fruits of international capitalism. But one could just as easily view globalization with trepidation, scepticism and criticism. The same computer systems that enable international navigation also destroy the skills and well-paid, unionized jobs of seafarers and dock workers. Bulk container shipping lines frequently sail under 'flags of convenience' – a practice whereby ocean-going vessels are registered in nations with the lowest safety, ecology and labour standards in order to boost profits, cut costs and evade inspections. I've used the word 'our' at the top of this paragraph, but who actually owns today's global capitalism? Critics ask who, if anyone, is in charge of regulating and policing it? Who are the winners and losers in this new game of global trade?

The huge literature on globalization therefore contains elements of awe, celebration and promotion, but also fear, concern and protestation. This theme – of the positive and negative elements of globalization being at once contradictory yet also somehow inseparable, perhaps even complementary – will be central to this book. Globalization can include democratic, progressive and modernizing elements. It is often associated with a dramatic increase in economic efficiency and with raising the general standard of living of the world's population. But opening up world markets and breaking down barriers to international trade also exposes nations, governments and citizens to new risks and entanglements. We can celebrate the complexity, variety, efficiency and technological sophistication of global markets. But we can also wring our hands at job losses, factory relocations, the rise of sweatshops, criminal networks, terrorism, drugs smuggling, arms trading and the sort of pointless consumerism seen at the supermarket deli counter before Christmas (Bozkurt, 2015).

Today's global population of 7 billion humans creates an estimated 4 billion tonnes of waste per year (Moses, 2013). Think of those same shipping containers making their return trip back to the Orient stuffed with trash for landfill disposal, to say nothing of the estimated 8 million tonnes of plastic waste clogging our oceans for decades to come. Much worse, every day on the world's sea, air, rail and roads, *human* traffic is present in thousands of trucks, buses, shipping containers and unseaworthy boats in the form of refugees and migrants. Some are trafficked by international criminal gangs (Nordstrom, 2007; Ritzer, 2010: 381–2). Tragically, the young, frail, sick, old or otherwise unfortunate often won't survive the journey. On arrival, refugees and migrants can expect further tribulations: paramilitary-style holding camps, processing through Kafka-esque nightmares of paperwork, security checks and work-permits. Families are separated. Migrants then scramble for work, housing and immigration status, often in the face of overt and covert racism and discrimination.

This constant swirl of physical, economic, financial and human traffic projects a fearsome muddle of international bureaucracy; who is responsible for this global web of people, products and movement in all its complexity and turmoil? Is globalization creating new forms of unity for humankind, or is it dividing people against themselves? Who is making sense of or trying to control this incessant change and disruption? Whose regulations are we supposed to be bound by? The compression of the world by new transportation technologies and the opening of economic borders arguably increases a sense of a world consciousness (Steger, 2013: 15) and an appreciation – sometimes sketchy – that global integration poses both risks and opportunities (Giddens, 1991). Mainstream, optimistic globalization theory tempts us to think about globalization as progressive, peaceful and unifying. But notions of a 'global personhood' or 'global community' (Steger, 2013: 15) are necessarily contested and uncertain things.

A possible illustrator of this is the story of a famous photograph taken by the crew of the NASA Apollo 8 spacecraft. It is a picture of a gloriously colourful planet Earth, much of it hidden by the inky blackness of space, somehow miraculously 'hanging' in the cosmos. Foregrounding the image is the barren Moon's surface. The Earth's exceptional vivacity is captured between the emptiness of deep space and the Moon's deathly hostility. The picture's official bureaucratic identifier, so beloved of government agencies such as NASA, is AS8-14-2383, but it is much better known by the more poetic *Earthrise*. Crammed into the 36 x 12 feet Command and Service Module, the three-man crew of Apollo 8 were the first humans to see the planet from this unique perspective. The shot was taken on 24 December 1968. Christmas Eve. It was the tail end of an extraordinary year in which mass public protests had broken out all over Europe and the USA; fierce conflict and debate over urgent issues of poverty, inequality, racism and war. The US itself was embroiled in a disastrous war in Vietnam, a centrepiece of the global Cold War standoff between the USA and its Western European allies versus the communist USSR and China. None of these conflicts could be seen from lunar orbit, but this photograph, and the later, equally famous NASA 'Blue Marble' image, hint at the fragility of a 'spaceship Earth' and a broader global consciousness that ought to protect the priceless planet and its warring, ecologically wasteful human occupants. The crew even read out a Christmas message to the millions of TV and radio listeners – the first ten verses of the Book of Genesis, which astronaut Jim Lovell suggested was:

> the foundation of many of the world's religions, not just the Christian religion. There are more people in other religions than the Christian religion around the world, and so this would be appropriate to that, and so that's how it came to pass.

They closed their broadcast with good wishes for everyone 'on the good Earth' (NASA, 2014).

Imagery and claims towards a 'world as one' are common to many forms of human imagination (political, religious, scientific, ecological, sporting, commercial, media and entertainment-related) yet are shot through with difference, confusion and conflict – something that Lovell maybe alludes to in his slightly awkward statement. While many would celebrate the Apollo space programme as one of the greatest scientific and cultural achievements of the Western world (see Parker, 2008), many critics – at the time of the Cold War and now – would see reflected in NASA and Lovell all-too-familiar manifestations of American capitalist arrogance and hypocrisy. Just as the Apollo programme reflected the might of US corporations such as Boeing, General Electric and Westinghouse, these same corporations were deeply implicated in US militarism and war profiteering. NASA astronauts were often elite aviators drawn from the US Air Force, Navy and Marine Corps. While an elite few were circling the globe in spacecraft and making claims about 'giant leaps for mankind' their brothers in arms were unleashing tonne upon tonne of napalm and high explosive on Vietnamese villages in the name of 'freedom' and 'liberty'. The United States' government, its corporations and its churches might sometimes take it upon themselves to speak for the world, but their influence and worldview are far from globally accepted and supported. Like 'globalization' itself, assertions by some nations, communities and political groups of a 'world in union' can be regarded by others as superficial, erroneous and demeaning.

This short book explores the various intermingled aspects that make up the processes and controversies of so-called 'globalization'. This rather ugly word has come to encapsulate a very wide range of substantive developments and debates and a broad spectrum of writings, theories, factoids and opinions. Much of the literature on globalization describes it as powerful, new, inexorable, and a force for good. Closer integration of the world is inevitable and unstoppable. It is pointless to oppose and self-defeating to try. This book will challenge such broadly held assumptions, introducing and discussing all kinds of counterpoints and perspectives that both affirm and challenge the assumptions that underpin globalization, inviting readers to develop their own positions on what precisely globalization might mean, both as a concept and as a set of 'really-existing' phenomena. Chapters will explore the history and rise of the concept; sceptical and critical ideas as regards globalization; the intense debates around the possible emergence of a global culture; and the implications of globalization for work, business, management and organization. The final chapter will explore the potential for the decline or even fall of globalization. Overall this book is a rapid dash journey through the theories, debates and manifestations of globalization, and of the lifecycle of the concept as it appears across various texts and perspectives.

1

Globalization – The Rise

Globalization is simultaneously an effect and a cause.

(Jan Aart Scholte, 2005: 4)

Globalization means different things to different people. It would probably be pointless (and treading a very well-worn path) to try to find a definition that works for everyone, especially given the broadness of a term that attempts to capture and explain forces, structures and processes that influence the whole of humanity. Many books on globalization start with a discussion of prior attempts to define the term (see, for example, Martell, 2010: 11–16, or Steger, 2013: 9–16), noting how globalization encompasses and influences a huge range of dimensions, including economic, cultural, political, linguistic and organizational. According to Ritzer (2010: 2):

> globalization is a transplanetary process or set of processes involving increasing liquidity and the growing multidirectional flows of people, objects, places and information as well as the structures they encounter and create that are barriers to, or expedite, those flows ...

This definition uses metaphors of movement and blockage, in keeping with other definitions which conceptualize globalization as the increased ability for people and processes to move and operate internationally or globally. Other famous globalization writers describe a metaphorical shrinkage of the world via technological, economic and political developments which somehow bring the population of the world into closer contact. These include the 'compression of the world and the intensification of the consciousness of the world as a whole' (Robertson, 1992: 8) and the 'intensification of worldwide social relations' (Giddens, 1991: 64). Although economics and international business clearly play a major role in globalization, the phenomenon is not solely about economics. Instead, globalization is a multifaceted set of phenomena that arguably influences almost all dimensions of life (Steger, 2013), making human society across the world increasingly interconnected and interdependent.

The term or concept of 'globalization' shot to prominence in the mid-to-late 1980s (Held et al., 1999: 1; Martell, 2007: 173). From around this point forward, the forces, processes and images of global integration seemed ubiquitous across the worlds of business, politics, academia, journalism and entertainment. They have arguably remained so ever since. To introduce the purpose and content of this book, this opening chapter explores the various meanings of the term, discusses where it came from, and begins to unpack some of its contested debates and interpretations.

Probably the most significant event that contextualizes the explosion of interest in 'globalization' is the end of the Cold War and the collapse of communism in Eastern Europe and the Soviet Union across 1989–91 (Ray, 2007: 3). These dramatic political and economic changes suggested a sudden and irrevocable opening of political and economic relations around much of the world. The political and economic doctrine of neoliberalism was in the ascendant, a doctrine described as '(1) an ideology; (2) a mode of governance; (3) a policy package' (Steger and Roy, 2010: 11). These three elements are central to the continual spread of the policies of 'market globalism' around the world and the rhetorical ways in which they are justified. Put simply, neoliberalism implies the expansion of global markets, free trade and commercial business activity and the occlusion of government, welfare and regulation. More competition equals less regulation. Freer markets means weakened states (Beck, 2000: 7).

Rapid technological advances in the fields of telecommunication, transportation and computing technologies throughout the 1980s onwards made international contact cheaper, easier, quicker, more interactive, more prevalent and more necessary. A bull market in the 1990s fuelled investor interest in technology and internet stocks, reinforcing notions of a radically new, digitized, 'weightless' economy of worldwide services, including so-called cultural and knowledge industries. Having 'won' the Cold War, political leaders in the West championed free markets and the spread of democracy but also worried about the new waves of global change that threatened government power and were difficult to regulate.

These separate yet interrelated areas of change reinforced one another. Dramatic political reform opened up new areas of the world to global markets and sent a rollercoaster ride of free-market capitalism to weave through the world economy including the hitherto sealed-off countries of the former Soviet Union. Triumphant right-wing commentators proclaimed the collapse of communism as 'the end of history' (Fukuyama, 1992) and a 'New World Order' (the latter notion a soundbite from US President George H.W. Bush's 1991 State of the Union address). Other communist nations (primarily China) accelerated their economic reforms towards encouraging ever-greater degrees of market forces, competition and international economic relations. New international markets, workforces and opportunities opened up in places such as India which also abandoned much of its socialist-leaning government planning and regulation of the economy (McCann, 2014a: 255–7). Physically and technically, economic globalization was enabled by improvements in computing architecture, processing speed and software design. The internet rapidly took on a central role in daily life, dramatically broadening, deepening and accelerating international communication and information spread. Stock exchanges became digitized and the rise of 'high-frequency trading' enabled and created the need for an acceleration of the pace of financial trading. Time is money after all.

Globalization created and reproduced itself in giant feedback loops that fed into further developments. Technological change, political change, economic change and cultural change all went hand-in-hand. Academic, media and political commentary fed this endless recursive loop. Writings on globalization, digitalization, financialization and a new world order were everywhere you looked. Universities scrambled to develop courses, degrees and departments dedicated to 'Global Studies'. New academic journals were founded, such as *Global Networks* (launched 2001), *Globalizations* (first volume 2004), and *Journal of Critical Globalisation Studies* (inaugurated 2009). Indeed, this book – like the notion of globalization itself (Giddens, 1999: 7) – is in some sense a product of the processes it describes.

The terms 'globalization', 'world economy' and 'global market forces' became catch-all buzzwords used by business leaders, politicians, media commentators and academics. Many of these opinion-leaders were members of a cosmopolitan global elite or 'transnational capitalist class' (Sklair, 2000) and tended to speak of globalization as something to praise, encourage and normalize. Certainly the first major 'wave' of globalization literature by authors such as Kenichi Ohmae and Thomas Freidman (see Held et al., 1999: 2–10; Martell, 2007) promulgated such a worldview as follows: growing international trade is generating more global and local wealth; standards of living are rising; autocratic governments have collapsed; the failed logics of communism, trade barriers and economic planning have been utterly discredited by the successes and dynamism of free markets; and the policies and doctrines of privatization and deregulation are rapidly – and rightly – spreading throughout the globe. These 'first wave' globalization texts, such as *The Borderless World* (Ohmae, 1991), *The Lexus and the Olive Tree* (Friedman, 1999) and *Going*

Global (Taylor and Webber, 1996) were simplistic in many ways and often the product of business journalists or current and former executives who unashamedly promoted neoliberal economic globalization with little in the way of historic, political or theoretical nuance. *Going Global* carries a gushing, highly corporate front cover endorsement by business consultant Tom Peters: 'Captures the spirit of the brave new times ... Nice job!'.

But that was the nineties – only the beginning of the globalization craze. In today's world of corporate 'superbrands', global value chains, nearly fifty thousand airports, cloud computing, the Indian Premier League, World of Warcraft, 2 billion Android users and Justin Bieber's 103 million Twitter followers, isn't globalization self-evident and now kind of boring? Hasn't the concept become old and hackneyed? What more can anyone possibly say on the subject?

The answer, I hope, is rather a lot. In a world of flux, change and disputed knowledge claims, where the next big idea often declines as rapidly as it appears, the globalization publishing and studying boom seems to defy gravity. Globalization remains an attractive area for studying, writing and publishing. A recent bestseller on globalization is Thomas Friedman's *The World is Flat* (2007) in which many familiar globalization arguments are repackaged in more up-to-date form, including the latest developments in internet technology and the rapid growth of outsourcing and offshoring. He uses the metaphor of 'Globalization 2.0', suggesting that times have moved on apace since the first wave of writings on globalization in the early to mid-1990s. Others continue to reassert the accuracy of 'first wave' globalization writings. In a 2017 newspaper discussion of Yuval Noah Harari's books *Sapiens* and *Homo Deus*, the physicist Helen Czerski suggests that, '[w]e are living through a fantastically rapid globalisation', and asks the author whether there will 'be one global culture in the future or will we maintain some sort of deliberate artificial tribal grouping?' Harari's answer:

> We'll probably have just one civilization. In a way this is already the case. All over the world the political system of the state is roughly identical. All over the world capitalism is the dominant economic system. [...] There are no longer any fundamental civilizational differences. (Anthony, 2017)

Francis Fukuyama, he concludes, 'was largely correct.'

Globalization as a concept has not become obvious and boring or died away; instead it has multiplied and mutated like a virus. Today there is no such thing as the 'globalization literature' that can be cross-sectioned, filleted and placed into a comparative table (like Held et al.

do in *Global Transformations*, 1999: 10). Contemporary writings on global society discuss *globalizations* in the plural, rather than *globalization* in the singular. Notions of globality have spiralled out into all kinds of disciplines and substantive areas. Long-established disciplines such as sociology, geography, politics, anthropology and history now also have to contend with globalization as a major part of their curriculum and methods of study.

Why is globalization such a pervasive phenomenon that continues to attract interest around 30 years after its rise to popularity? There are probably several reasons for this. Firstly, a significant part of the explanation surely resides in the ways in which globalization is still so strongly promoted as correct and inevitable, much like the assertive first wave literature that talks of the triumph of free markets and democracy – a kind of market fundamentalism (Frank, 2001). It is far from surprising that multinational corporations, politicians and think tanks all promote the ideology of globalization and global integration as it is clearly in their interests to do so. A global transnational class stands to gain from promoting, justifying and normalizing global markets, global communities, global cultural consumption and global imaginaries (Sklair, 2000; Steger, 2013; Steger and Roy, 2010).

But this can't explain all of the enduring popularity of globalization. The vast majority of the global population is not, of course, part of the elite, and is often far from convinced that their own interests are going to coincide so happily with those of the global free marketeers. As we shall see in much more depth in the next two chapters there are also plenty of sceptical and critical writers on globalization. But, interestingly, these writings also seem to somehow promote and sustain the notion of globalization rather than debunking it entirely. Anti-globalists, or those promoting 'justice globalism' or even 'jihad globalism' tend also to construct their worldview in terms of big-picture 'global' issues and, in so doing, add to the breadth and range of writings that make up the ever-expanding canon of literature framed at the level of the global imaginary (see Steger, 2013). I will turn to these ideas in more depth in the following two chapters and I will discuss the controversy surrounding the use of the term 'jihad' in globalization studies in Chapter 4. But for now, it is safe to say that over time globalization literatures (or globalizations in the plural) have expanded and developed in a universe of different directions. Much of the straightforward optimism and boastfulness of the 1980s–1990s' globalization literature now looks misplaced, naïve and vulgar. Globalization doesn't just mean the increasing spread of markets and democracy. It also implies transnational terrorist networks, rising international economic inequality, environmental catastrophe, economic crises, political scandals and the collapse of public trust in the 'progress' and 'democracy' promoted by our global political and business leaders. Contemporary globalizations imply increasing heterodoxy and chaos; the rapidly accelerating unmanageability of global affairs (Guillén, 2015; Virilio, 2012a, 2012b).

Enthusiasts for globalization face their mirror image in a broad range of critics and sceptics. Far from representing a new world order of economic, political and cultural integration, globalization also became an umbrella term for a range of serious risks, evils and grievances. The early globalist literature was soon confronted by critics such as George Ritzer's McDonaldization thesis (Ritzer, 2014; first edition 1993), in which the logic of economic and cultural globalization is symbolized by the unhealthy, restrictive and culturally dumbed-down management systems of McDonald's fast-food outlets. Concurrently, globalization sceptics such as Hirst and Thompson (2001), Rosenberg (2000) and Veseth (2010) were arguing that globalization is an exaggerated and mythological concept, with much of the world isolated from supposedly 'global' flows or networks. These debates have refused to settle since the nineties, as shown by the frequent re-issuing of classic globalization texts such as *McDonaldization* (Ritzer, 2014), *Jihad vs. McWorld* (Barber, 2011) and *Globalization in Question* (Hirst et al., 2009).

These controversies have only been deepened by the calamitous events of the 2000s, such as the 9/11 terrorist attacks and the so-called 'War on Terror'; the second Iraq War and prolonged counterinsurgency campaigns that have bogged down Western militaries; revelations about state-sponsored electronic snooping; the subprime mortgage fiasco that triggered a massive financial downturn in 2007–10; increasingly disquieting evidence about global warming and climate change; and other developments that possibly signal a reversal or at the very least a problematizing of globalization (such as the UK voting in a referendum in June 2016 to leave the European Union). *The Independent* newspaper in 2011 editorialized about the 2000s as 'a lost decade' in which the unifying forces of globalization hit the buffers or reversed course (Cornwell, 2011).

But such is the perverse logic of globalization as a discourse or field that these localizing, anti-globalist or de-globalizing tendencies are somehow brought into the globalization stable and become part of its seedbed. You believe in it even as you deny it. You are for it even when against it. Globalization cannot be a singular theory or even a distinct literature. It is like some kind of conceptual vacuum cleaner, hoovering up ideas, criticisms and scepticism, claiming all as parts of itself under the broader global brand or narrative. Globalization as a concept or set of writings actually reflects what it claims – globalization is inescapable and unavoidable. It knows what's good for you. It's a bit like the war cry of those horrid galactic imperialists 'The Borg' in the science-fiction franchise *Star Trek*: 'resistance is futile' (Klikauer, 2013: 73; Veseth, 2010: 8).

In some sense, therefore, the breadth of the term 'globalization' and its dramatic manifestation as utopia or dystopia (or both) is precisely what makes the term and field of study attractive. It is both compelling and repulsive, like The Borg. This horror/intensity trope is often what international news media play to when portraying globalization. It is epitomized perhaps by the dreadful imagery of the 9/11 attacks: planes and explosions ripping through the twin towers of the World Trade Center, panicking citizens running down New York streets pursued by cascading walls of dust. It is also precisely the images that global terrorist organizations want to see broadcast around the world. Terror, risk and states of emergency have become routine. Globalization's unruliness, breadth, unpredictability, adaptability and ability to reinvent and mutate are clearly important reasons why it refuses to die as a concept or genre of writing.

Globalization is therefore a popular academic field of study simply because it gives us something big and brash to play with. It can be used as shorthand to describe almost any process or outcome, any cause or effect, depending on one's political taste. It signifies everything and nothing (Bauman, 1998; Ritzer, 2007). Globalization's very grandiosity, especially in a time of general scepticism about grand theories (James and Steger, 2014), gives us a welcome free-for-all, a wild and wacky playground inside the academic precincts which tend instead towards granular detail, conservatism and precision. The globalization literature is certainly dumbed-down in places. On the other hand, global studies is a place for 'big picture' analysis, where connections can be made between an array of disciplines and where boundaries and problems can be rethought and redrawn.

Some have attacked the likes of George Ritzer for the simplicity and commerciality of their globalization writings, claiming that kind of work precisely reflects the intellectual poverty, 'nothingness' and crass commercialism of McDonaldization and globalization itself. Roberts (2005) describes this process as the 'Ritzerization' of knowledge. Globalization – *I'm Lovin' It*. Some otherwise highly cerebral writers have tended towards dumbing-down in producing another blockbuster globalization text. Anthony Giddens, one of the most prominent sociologists of the 1990s and early 2000s, devoted a considerable portion of his latter career to exploring various global themes, and many would say that his outputs became increasingly simplistic in the process. Here, in *Runaway World*, he ruminates on globalization in a way that reflects his own high status as a cosmopolitan elite commentator:

I travel a lot to speak abroad. I haven't been to a single country recently where globalisation isn't being intensively discussed. In France, the word is *mondialisation*. In Spain and Latin America, it is *globalizacion*. The Germans say *Globalisierung*. (Giddens, 1999: 7)

Globalization creates a trend whereby an author's theoretical contribution is promoted up the ranks, so to speak; transposed upwards from a regional or national idea to being some kind of global phenomenon, almost as a manager rises up a corporation from divisional director to 'global head of sales'. So, for Ulrich Beck, we go from *Risk Society* (1992) to *World Risk Society* (1999) and *World at Risk* (2008). Concepts are expanded 'up and out' from the local and national to the global and international. The theory is supposedly equally applicable everywhere.

Beck is most famous for his 'risk society' thesis. Themes of risk, lack of control and a desire for management dominate globalization writings such as *Runaway World* (Giddens, 1999). They reflect a profound schizophrenia and anxiety about globalization that reside in all of these largely pro-globalist texts from the 1990s onwards. Globalization is largely inevitable and broadly a good thing but no-one is in control of it. The timing of these writings perhaps reflect pre-millennial tensions, but notions of risk, crisis, unpredictability and fear have never been far from the surface of globalization writings ever since. Globalization needs managing but is not very amenable to management. High-profile global theorists such as Giddens are not just simple-minded globalization-promoters but are also at least partial critics of the phenomenon.

Dumbed-down or not, globalization as a concept seems somehow to tap into a sense of ever-growing world connectedness – what Steger (2006) calls 'global imaginaries'. In other words, it fits the zeitgeist. Globalization writings reflect how many people regard the contemporary world: viewing change and development as exciting but also confusing and frightening. Life in the twenty-first century often seems fast-paced, ever-changing, unpredictable and rampantly consumerist. The globalization literature captures this sense of 'totality' of the effects of free market capitalism on human society (see Jay, 1992). The phraseology of globalization remains very current. In the summer of 2016, former UK Prime Minister Gordon Brown placed an article in *The Financial Times* arguing that 'leaders must make the case for globalisation' following Britain's highly controversial vote to exit from the European Union (2016). At the heart of this notion of globalization lies a vague yet powerful image of mysterious global forces that are bigger than those of 'the nation state' and reach deeply into all of our lives. Its totality (and lack of clarity) mean that it can be used – like a religion or ideology – to apply to almost any debate or discussion; it seems current, it seems urgent. It is something that many of us somehow sense on a daily basis.

For all of the above reasons, the notion of globalization has continued to grow since the 1980s. Now would be a good time to trace its rise and scope.

The fad that refuses to die: Tracking the rise and rise of globalization

According to Ritzer (2010: xv) globalization 'entered the lexicon only three decades ago'. For Held and colleagues, it is 'an idea whose time has come. From obscure origins in French and American writings in the 1960s, the concept of globalization finds expression today in all the world's major languages' (Held et al., 1999: 1). Many introductory globalization texts ruminate about the term's sudden and rapid emergence. Google's Ngram Viewer is a tool that searches Google's enormous repository of digitized books in English. Searching 'globalization' (and the alternate spelling 'globalisation') confirms the widely held view that the word barely existed until the early 1980s and that its usage suddenly boomed from then on. As Figure 1.1 demonstrates, the usage is still climbing. Although the curve tapers off somewhat in the most recent years, there are probably good reasons to predict another

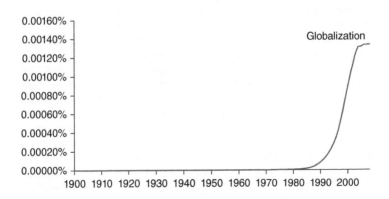

FIGURE 1.1

Source: Google Ngram Viewer (http://books.google.com/ngrams)

rise to come soon (see King, 2017). This is because globalization has very much returned to contemporary prominence; populist, nationalist politicians such as Donald Trump, Marine Le Pen and Nigel Farage position themselves as defenders of ordinary people who have been 'left behind' by globalization and are typically ignored or patronized by cosmopolitan, globalist elites.

Although Figure 1.1 suggests a sudden and rapid growth of the concept, it would be rash to claim that globalization as a concept or phenomenon has 'come from nowhere to be almost everywhere' (Giddens, 1999: 7). James and Steger (2014) provide a detailed and intriguing 'career of the concept', suggesting globalization is 'one of the most important concepts for understanding the passage of human society into the third millennium' (2014: 418). The earliest reference they found to 'globalization' was actually in 1930, although the word at that point was used with a different meaning from that of today, referring then to learning processes (2014: 425–6). In 1943 the US Presidential candidate Wendell Willkie published an optimistic book entitled *One World* that envisaged the nations of the planet cooperating and integrating once the Second World War ends. 'The world has become small and completely interdependent', he wrote (Greider, 1997: 16). Similarly, Scholte (2005: 16) suggests that self-styled 'scientific humanists' Oliver Reiser and Blodwen Davies coined the verb 'to globalize' in their book *Planetary Democracy* in 1944. James and Steger find sporadic references to 'globalization' in the late 1960s and early 1970s in which the term started to emerge with today's meaning. The most notable is probably by the political scientist George Modelski who sounds ahead of his time in describing 'the increasing size, complexity, and sophistication of world society' (as quoted in James and Steger, 2014: 427). It is a testament to the grandiosity, breadth and ubiquity of the term 'globalization' that no one writer has ever dared lay claim to having coined it. Note also the contradiction: the world has 'become small' (Willkie) yet 'world society' is increasing in size (Modelski)!

James and Steger also use Google Ngram to make their point visually. But a tool such as this can also be used to suggest that globalization is considerably less important than other central notions in human society, such as family, God or war. In fact, compared to the combined mass of writings on those particular themes, globalization seems irrelevant (see Figure 1.2). It is probably the case that much of the world's population would agree that it lives in some kind of 'global age' (Albrow, 1996), and can recognize the 'intensification of consciousness of the world as a whole' (Robertson, 1992: 8), or a 'global imaginary'

(Steger, 2013: 10). But it is vital to remember that global forces do not invade, change and structure literally everything in life. In many senses, community, locality, tradition, culture and language can be highly distinctive from others elsewhere and can be vital ingredients of identity and everyday life.

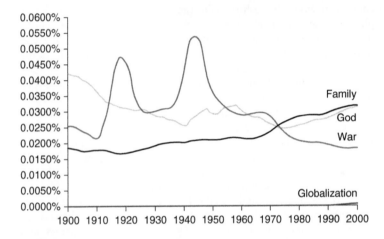

FIGURE 1.2

Source: Google Ngram Viewer (http://books.google.com/ngrams)

Globalization is unclear and hard to define. Mittelman (2000) calls it a 'syndrome'. For Bauman, it's a 'shibboleth' or even 'magic incantation' (1998: 1). To some it seems faddish, superficial, too broad and contradictory to make any real sense. One might imagine, therefore, that globalization as a concept might die off, much like other fads (see Birnbaum, 2000). So far that hasn't happened, suggesting there is something enduring and useful about the concept (Ferguson and Mansbach, 2012; Thompson, 2014: 1). Its usage has increased and its area and scope have broadened. While often declared to be vitally important, globalization is also confounded by 'hesitation, vagueness and inconsistency' (Scholte, 2005: 1). It is extremely difficult to define globalization but it is possible to explore the various approaches and perspectives that constitute its literature. By way of introduction to the rest of the book, let us explore some of these perspectives in turn. The three that feature most heavily in this book are globalization as an economic, cultural or political debate.

Globalization as an economic debate

Most mainstream or common-sense discussions of globalization focus primarily on its economic dimensions. But within this economic frame of reference there are many competing versions of what economic globalization is and what it does. The mainstream position is that globalization is a set of largely inevitable and progressive processes, explainable by concepts derived from the discipline of economics, where abstract 'laws' of supply and demand dominate and where prices and markets cannot be wrong or problematic in any significant way. Globalization is described as an inexorable force for good; it creates wealth and jobs, boosts connectivity and increases the technological sophistication and efficiency of everyday life. It brings world trade together to enhance the greatest happiness of the greatest number. It is impossible to resist it, and in any case there is no point resisting as its processes and outcomes are good for all people. Prominent examples include the *Financial Times* journalist Martin Wolf (2004) and economist Jagdish Bhagwati (2007). This optimistic view is, of course, bitterly contested by those who are critical of economic globalization, focusing on the ruthless behaviour of giant corporations which can run roughshod over democratic governance and regulation in their pursuit of profit. Critics lament the increasing precariousness of jobs and careers, growing wealth inequality and the widespread exploitation and poverty that most of the world's population has to contend with. Many of the critics of economic globalization have socialist or Marxist backgrounds and sympathize with those who organize to resist globalization or at least develop more democratic and humanist policy responses, such as trade unions, human rights and poverty-reduction campaigners, or charities such as War on Want (Chomsky, 2012; Klein, 2010; Stiglitz, 2007).

Further economic debates around globalization continue to emerge as the world economy generates rapid change and is in turn enveloped by it. Since the 1970s, the volume of world trade and foreign direct investment has grown rapidly, rebounding from periodic shocks and crises. A wide range of transnational political governance organizations have been established as part of international efforts to try to regulate and manage global trade, development, labour and finance, such as the International Monetary Fund (IMF), World Trade

Organization (WTO), International Labour Organization (ILO) and United Nations Conference on Trade and Development (UNCTAD). Treaties negotiated between national governments have aimed to reduce trade barriers; harmonize taxes; set ecological and labour standards; and establish shared legal structures to reduce the costs and confusions of international economic activity. In practice, these have often been murderously complicated and politically contentious, such as the Uruguay and Doha Rounds of WTO negotiations that have been problematic for decades; the North American Free Trade Agreement of the 1990s; the proposed Trans-Pacific Partnership (TPP); the Comprehensive Economic and Trade Agreement (CETA); and the Transatlantic Trade and Investment Partnership (TTIP). However complex, frustrating and ineffective, the broad policy direction has been obvious – towards the growing international integration and harmonization of economic activity. Whether this integration actually helps to serve the interests of the majority of the world's population or whether it serves to further line the pockets of the elites and global corporations while weakening national governments and making employment more precarious is another matter.

Much has also been made of how economic globalization 'opens up' new regions of the world to global economic trade. There is a voluminous literature on the recent economic growth of 'sleeping giants' such as so-called 'BRICs' of Brazil, Russia, India and China who for some time have been 'emerging' as major economic powers in their own right. It is interesting to note how the coining of the term 'BRIC' was attributed to the former Goldman Sachs economist and British Conservative cabinet minister Jim O'Neill. While parts of the world are certainly growing it says a lot about the enduring power of Western 'global' media that it takes a member of the Western elite to provide the 'approval' of the economic progress made by countries encompassing nearly 3 billion people. Goldman Sachs analysts have more recently come up with 'MINT' (Mexico, Indonesia, Nigeria and Turkey) and the 'Next 11': Bangladesh, Egypt, Indonesia, Iran, Mexico, Nigeria, Pakistan, Philippines, Turkey, South Korea and Vietnam. Such countries are praised by the global investment community for their 'effective macroeconomic policies' and 'political stability'. For proponents of economic globalization, the rapid development of formerly weak economies into major powers is a valuable part of their argument. They claim that free trade and global economic integration has resulted in a huge reduction in global poverty, with perhaps a billion people 'lifted out' of extreme hardship in recent decades (Bhagwati, 2007). Globalization is working, they argue, and people in the developing world want more of it. What they *don't* need is Western bleeding-heart liberals or socialists claiming to speak for them by advocating more regulation and restraints of global economic trade.

Other elements of the debates associated with economic globaliza-tion include the rise and evaluation of global brands (often into groups or league tables, much like countries); the decline of mass industry and its replacement by service economies in many parts of the world; and the growing importance of intangibles such as image, information and data. There is much talk of a knowledge economy, creative economy, or otherwise 'weightless' economy in which traditional skills that built and sustained industrial capitalism are now redundant. With manufacturing plants shuttered in the advanced economies of Europe, USA and Japan, jobs in these regions are more likely to be found in the white-collar occupations of the service sector: banking, healthcare, education, con-sulting, information and communication industries. These are well-paid, intrinsically interesting jobs relying on highly qualified labour. Unfortunately, of course, not everyone will have the skills, abilities and opportunities to work in such areas, and will be confined to the large number of low-skilled, precarious and 'dead-end' jobs that service economies create: retail, shelf-stacking, security guards, cleaning. According to Ritzer:

> Prior to the current epoch of globalization [...] one of the things that characterized people, things, information, places, and much else was their greater solidity. [...] [P]eople didn't move very far, neither did information. [...] However, at an increasing rate over the last few centuries, and especially in the last several decades, that which one seemed so solid has tended to 'melt' and become increasingly *liquid*. (Ritzer, 2010: 4–5)

In terms of work and jobs, formerly 'solid' jobs, such as those in the manufacturing industries, were fixed in place and could be expected to be relatively secure and enduring. And today? Not so much. In a global environment of 'liquid modernity' (Bauman, 2000), manufacturing labour can be readily replaced or eradicated. Electronically enabled services can increasingly be delivered remotely from where the end-users place their orders. Radical improvements in communications and information technologies have enabled certain services to be traded overseas, such as customer contact centres and back-office processing work being performed in India, a process known as 'offshoring' or 'business process outsourcing' (BPO). While some services are physi-cally bounded – you can't offshore a haircut – the message of Friedman and others is clear. If new global digital communication technologies are ushering in the 'death of distance' (Cairncross, 2001) and making the world 'flat' (Friedman, 2007), then many types of service industry become increasingly vulnerable to being moved overseas to low-cost, low-regulation environments, just like manufacturing industries have been for decades. Economist Alan Blinder (2006) estimated that as many as 28–42 million US jobs could potentially be lost to offshoring. It is not only the most basic work such as telephone call handling that is moving overseas. We've also seen well-paid, middle class, often unionized white-collar work such as actuarial services, publishing or human resource management moving to overseas back-office providers (McCann, 2014b; Taylor and Bain, 2005). University lectures and seminars are replaced by online downloadable 'interactive content'. Globalization's effects on work and careers can be bewildering, with ever-increasing fears and insecurities about the future. How safe can any job be if it bobs along on the 'flows' of a 'weightless' economy with no means of controlling its own direction?

In many ways, the economic frame of reference sees globalization as simply another word for global capitalism; debates about globalization's economic effects are mostly interchangeable with those relating to the nature of global capitalism. Clearly influencing contemporary writers such as Ritzer and Bauman, Karl Marx and Friedrich Engels wrote in 1848 in their *Manifesto of the Communist Party* that '[A]ll that is solid melts into air'. Chapter 3 of this book will explore these economic controversies in depth, and Chapter 5 will also explore how the broad economic dimensions of globalization also affect and structure the more everyday features of management, organization and work, for better and for worse.

Globalization as a cultural debate

A second major area of globalization discussion surrounds the issue of global culture. Most of the globalization authors insist that globalization is not solely an economic phenomenon and must be considered as something much broader and complex, filtering into every part of human society (see Steger, 2013). Again, as with economic debates in globalization, views are split as to how globalization influences and structures culture and what role culture plays in globalization – causes, effects and relationships between culture and globalization are certainly present, but hard to delineate and make sense of. It doesn't help that the term 'culture' is just as hard to define as globalization. But generally 'culture' refers to social traditions, rituals and behaviours that structure, define and constitute society, such as language, religion, clothing and food, as well as spoken and unspoken norms around everyday and taken-for-granted institutions such as 'the family'. It can also encompass physical or non-physical creations that can be experienced, viewed, read, worn, watched, or played, and is increasingly developed and sold commercially. It includes cultural products derived from the entertainment industry, including film, TV, publishing, music, fashion, video games and suchlike. The increased 'liquidity' of globalization implies the potentially rapid diffusion, consumption and adaptation of cultural products at ever greater speed through various digital communication platforms.

On one level, the connection of globalization to culture is obvious, relating directly to the increasing globalization of the culture industry or entertainment industry. The power of global entertainment brands such as those owned by the Disney Corporation or the role of US fast-food restaurants are obvious manifestations of the global culture industry, discussed at length in the globalization literature (see Bryman, 1999; Ritzer, 2014). There is also considerable debate around 'traditional', 'foreign' or 'local' cultures in terms of how they might interact with, accept, adapt, or reject 'global' (typically Anglo-American) corporate cultural products. For many, Western-led globalization poses a challenge to local traditions and appears inauthentic, unwelcome and threatening. Benjamin Barber's (2011) writings on the broad theme of what he calls *Jihad vs. McWorld* are an important reflection of the ways in which the global culture industry – through its increasingly powerful international intrusion – also stimulates (and in fact enables) significant forms of local critique and pushback. The fear of being overwhelmed by an unwelcome, empty and frivolous global pop-culture creates a dynamic whereby local culture aggressively reasserts itself in response. Globalization reinforces nationalism or local traditionalism just as it overrides and erodes it. While some discussions of global culture or a 'global village' are constructed in terms of the progressive erosion of local and traditional forms of human culture, others see new forms of cultural hybridity, interaction and multiculturalism, as well as the reassertion of traditional forms of culture and social identity (Nederveen Pieterse, 1995; Wang and Yeh, 2005). 'Liquid modernity' is again implicated here. Digital technologies and the increased availability of bandwidth enables the creation and spread of alternative, home-made, low-budget, or crowdsourced cultural products that can challenge, compete with, emulate, rip off and satirize the huge market penetration of Hollywood film studios, corporate broadcasting and publishing or state-run monopoly 'public service' media providers. Chapter 4 will explore these complex and emotive 'global culture' debates in more depth.

Globalization as a political debate

A third major area of debate concerns how globalization is managed and controlled. Who might try to control it? By what means? And for whose interests? Broadly this is the debate around political globalization or 'global governance'. A very common trope in the globalization literature suggests that the increasingly 'liquid' manifestations of global society are ever-harder to control, and that globalization threatens and erodes the power and influence of the nation state in particular (Badiou, 2016: 23–4; Bauman, 1998: 55–76; Held, 1991; Held et al., 1999; Martell, 2010: 188–213). National governments of, for example, France, Malaysia, Turkey or even the United States, have less influence than the various forces and flows of globalization. States are becoming increasingly impotent in the face of global forces such as international migration, global warming, corporate expansion and terrorist and criminal networks.

The more mainstream political literature on globalization tends to claim that globalization certainly creates new economic, financial, social, cultural, legal and humanitarian challenges, but these are being generally quite 'effectively managed' at the level of national governments and perhaps more so by the complex new architecture of transnational government organizations such as the UN, the International Labour Organization, the International Criminal Court, and the World Bank. These institutions (many of which began life at the Bretton Woods conference at the end of the Second World War) have played key roles in governing and representing the world community at a multilateral level. This is global governance 'from above'. Such a 'macro' form of governance is increasingly supplemented by the development of more 'grass roots' organizations that make up 'global civil society': non-governmental organizations (NGOs), charities, pressure groups and social enterprises across every conceivable social issue, such as women's rights; HIV and AIDS; environmental protection; chronic poverty; food and water security; child soldiers; religious tolerance; migration; education and social work; access to healthcare; prison reform. This is global governance 'from below'. The mainstream narrative on global governance both from 'above' and 'below' is of progress, harmonization, integration and the general spread of economic and social wellbeing, being cautiously managed by professional and democratic transnational experts and influenced by socially concerned pressure groups (Kaldor, 2015; Keane, 2003). This all speaks to the notion of 'supraterritoriality' (Scholte, 2005) – the growing power of international political, cultural or economic influences that transcend national boundaries and operate largely independently of national governments.

Others dispute such a Panglossian interpretation, emphasizing instead the chaotic and unmanaged (perhaps unmanageable) nature of global networks and flows, suggesting that the post-Second World War Bretton Woods institutions such as the World Bank are incapable of handling the complexity and turmoil of contemporary global change. In many ways they probably exacerbate these problems by, for example, loading 'developing' countries with insurmountable debt burdens and forcibly opening up their economies to global free trade before they are really ready to compete internationally (Chang, 2003; Glennie, 2008). Global civil society is similarly ineffective in practice (Scholte, 2005: 367–71), often lacking influence, funding and access to corporate and political leadership.

Perhaps worse, some would claim that so-called 'global' civil society is a sham. Its organizations claim to represent the weak, the marginalized, those vulnerable to global or local social problems. But critics would claim that these charities and activists are re-enacting the 'white man's burden' of colonial days by interfering in matters they poorly understand and diverting attention away from global problems created by the West itself. Global civil society allows privileged white middle class westerners to save the turtles or teach a bit of English to orphans in Malawi for a couple of weeks, while their own nations' governments pursue disastrous wars on terror or wars on drugs, or prop up brutal, undemocratic regimes. Westerners can enjoy their 'Certified Fair Trade' food and drink while their taxes pay for tariff barriers that protect American or EU farmers from African, South American and Asian competitors. All the while, rich nations continue to receive interest payments from loans made to heavily indebted, less-developed countries in the 1960s–1980s.

An interesting backlash against global civil society activism erupted over the 'Kony 2012' campaign, based around a very well-marketed video produced by a civil society outfit known as Invisible Children. It focused on Joseph Kony, a brutal paramilitary cult leader allegedly responsible for a string of war crimes in Uganda and neighbouring states. The campaign pressed for increased US or UN military intervention to assist Ugandan forces in apprehending Kony so that he can face charges of war crimes and crimes against humanity at the International Criminal Court in The Hague. The video is a kind of tribute to the values of Western-led globalization and the wonders of social media. To its supporters the 30-minute film informed an ignorant West of an horrific war barely reported in mainstream media and was a powerful call to action, itself enabled by global technologies and an emerging global consciousness. Social media has informed us of this crisis so we now can't sit on our hands and do nothing to help. It was watched and recirculated by millions in the West, especially by young people in the USA forwarding and 'liking' the video on social media platforms. TV and film celebrities such as Oprah Winfrey, Angelina Jolie and P Diddy joined the campaign calling for increased military intervention in Uganda. Across the USA 'action kits' and 'stop Kony' wristbands sold in their thousands.

To critical observers #Kony2012 seemed insufferably smug, crass and self-indulgent. It emerged that the video contained numerous factual inaccuracies. Critics described the campaign as a media circus portraying Kony as pantomime villain and Ugandan children as victims crying out for American rescue in what is in reality a protracted conflict that few outside Uganda understand and in which Kony – grotesque as he is – is a relatively minor player (Devereaux, 2012). The campaign showed precious little effort to understand the deep complexities of the conflict or the broader contexts of war and poverty in this region or others. The insurgency in northern Uganda is one of many New Wars (Kaldor, 2012) or 'wars among the people' that cannot be understood in some reductionist way as the evils of one person. But forget all that. Self-righteous supporters could press on and save the world one wristband at a time. Invisible Children was ultimately subjected to a battery of protest and derision, with one critic labelling Kony 2012 and its ilk part of a 'White-Savior Industrial Complex' (Cole, 2012). Many others have criticized the concept of a 'global civil society' and its attempts to heal the world's ills as both hypocritical and ill-informed (Kumar, 2007; Munck, 2002).

To be fair to the ideals of civil society of global governance, many new problems faced by governments and their citizens are by nature transnational or borderless (such as cybercrime; international financial crises; disease pandemics; global warming; insurgency; genocide; and people trafficking). These require much greater international coordination and collaboration than national or transnational authorities have so far shown. It can hardly be said, for example, that multinational organizations such as the EU have got any kind of grip on the migrant crisis that has been a high-profile tragedy for decades. The global financial crisis of 2007–8 was also badly mishandled by national and international regulatory agencies which seemed complacent about or complicit in the increasing recklessness and greed of much of the world's banking, insurance and credit-rating industries. While there is an influential UN-established Intergovernmental Panel on Climate Change, its reports and warnings about global climate change are routinely sidelined or ignored by governments and corporations who think primarily about their own selfish, short-term needs (Giddens, 2011). International disease pandemics such as SARS or the Zika virus also cause logistical problems as the ease of international travel increases the speed at which disease vectors can infect the world's population. Cybercrime, identity theft and intellectual property rights violations are other major threats often said to operate at a 'global' level, thereby beyond the reach of local or national law enforcement. Risks and panics of disease, crime, ecological disaster, and terrorism are probably inflated by the technologies and practices of globalization, such as 24/7 rolling news and the incessant proliferation of homemade social media on platforms such as Twitter and Instagram (Furedi, 2006). Increased fear is in itself a threat or risk. While it is widely accepted that globalization challenges and threatens nation states and national governments, trans-national organizations and 'global civil society' often seem equally feeble in their attempts to manage and mitigate the risks and threats caused by increased global integration.

We have returned to the notion of global risk as a central issue across all perspectives of the globalization literature. Amid the optimistic accounts that global market forces and global civil society are ushering in a new era of openness, integration and democracy, come a range of writings portraying a lack of control, of systemic and unmanageable risks, and the absence of democratic accountability (Greider, 1997). Complexity, speed of change and lack of clarity surrounds globally traded services, meaning that the traders are often several steps ahead of the regulators. This applies equally to the internationalization of legal goods and services (such as financial derivatives) but also the obviously dangerous, base and criminal networks in narcotics, people smuggling, gun-running and child sexual exploitation (Ferguson, 2006; Nordstrom, 2007). The openness and interconnectivity of globalization means that international loopholes can be easily exploited, in both legal and extra-legal ways. This includes registering ocean-going vessels under flags of convenience (as we've seen in the Introduction), domiciling a company's head office in a low-tax zone, or passing billions of dollars of financial transactions through tiny offshore territories such as the Cayman Islands (Fichtner, 2014). National and transnational authorities may claim they are winning their 'wars' on drugs, crime, terrorism or aggressive tax planning, but scepticism about their progress and competence in these matters is probably well-founded.

Globalization is an enormous field of study and the above is simply my brief introduction to what I have chosen as the main areas of debate that a book of this length can reasonably be narrowed to: globalization as economic, cultural and political. We can already see why globalization is such an enduring and popular concept in that it goes well beyond the subjects of economics, business and management. Globalization is so multifaceted that it becomes relevant to almost all elements of society and culture, including education, sports, news, health, film and entertainment. Of course, all of these categories are businesses to some degree. But, more than this, the forces and concepts of globalization are widely understood to reach into and affect many elements of everyday life. Indeed, our everyday actions to some extent actually bring it into being (Ray, 2007). This makes globalization's influences upon us (whether benign or threatening) both recognizable and infinitely contentious.

Debates without end: What to expect from the rest of this book

We have seen how globalization is multifaceted in practice and its literature extremely diverse and splintered. Economically we have those who believe globalization is inevitable, efficient and just, and those who see it as exploitative, reckless and unfair. Some see global culture in terms of increasing hybridity and multiculturalism, whereas others accuse globalization of trampling on and destroying non-mainstream or subaltern cultures. Optimistic and mainstream pro-globalist writings describe the establishment of complex and effective new forms of transnational, global governance that are effectively dealing with planetary risks. Critics don't recognize this picture and declare 'global civil society' a myth. From their point of view an emerging world society is a chaotic place of new risks and crises that is weakly overseen by political and corporate elites that pursue their own narrow, self-interested agendas.

Literatures on globalization thus implicitly or explicitly have in mind the kind of world that their authors hope to see emerge. This entails not one vision of globalization, but many. Steger (2013: 103–30) identifies three different visions: 'market globalism', 'justice globalism' and 'religious globalism'. Market globalism promotes mainstream notions of free markets, deregulation and open competition in integrating the world through the spreading of capitalism and democracy. Justice globalism is the viewpoint of the wide variety of critics of market globalism who describe the exploitative and unfair elements of global capitalism. Religious globalism similarly rejects Western, market-led globalism and instead advocates that religious ideology should be the primary basis upon which world society should be united. To various degrees, religious globalism (or so-called 'jihad globalism') opposes secular notions of capitalism and representative democracy, sometimes violently (see also Barber, 1992; 2011).

In covering these debates in the following chapters I aim for the book to give full voice to the emotive and colourful debates that run through the huge and varied globalization literature. I hope the reader will enjoy this rather rapid dash through the dense thickets of debate and, having reached the end will be inclined to continue to explore these themes and literatures in the real depth that they deserve. If that is how it works out, then this short book will have done the job I had in mind for it to do. But hold on a minute. Before we get into these heated discussions of what globalization does, how it can be managed and whether its effects are for good or ill, there is another major debate about globalization that we have to settle accounts with first. This is the important view put forward by the 'second wave' globalization writers – the globalization sceptics. We explore their ideas in Chapter 2.

2

Globalization as Myth and Hype: Exploring the Globalization Sceptics

> Globalization exists as a process, but it is less complete than many people think and of a different nature than is commonly assumed.
>
> (Veseth, 1998: 188)

Try to imagine the worst place in the world. Where would it be? A hospital ward short of staff and supplies in a war-torn middle-eastern city? A collective farm in North Korea? An urban ghetto ravaged by drugs, gang crime and deindustrialization? Travel writer and *Sunday Times* journalist A.A. Gill once reserved the title 'worst place in the world' for an entire geographic region: the 'autonomous republic' of Karakalpakstan (Gill, 2005: 106). It sounds like the name of a made-up country in a Hollywood action movie full of extremists who hate our freedoms. But, no, it is actually real. It is a large territory in western Uzbekistan, an area struggling mightily with the disastrous legacy of the Soviet system and suffering a protracted nightmare of post-communist economic stagnation and political repression. I'd not heard of the place until I read Daniel Metcalfe's *Out of Steppe*, an entertaining book about the 'lost peoples' of Central Asia. In Nukus, the capital of Karakalpakstan, life seemed stripped of all motion and action. It's like someone's pressed 'pause' on the whole city and then wandered off with the remote control. He writes that 'in Nukus people didn't really walk. Old men lounged on shaded steps, child cigarette-sellers sat listlessly by their cartons' (Metcalfe, 2009: 25). The countryside appears even worse: 'The only landmarks were telephone poles and undulating wires. [...] This was a dirty beige nothingness, where sky met land in an underwhelming blur. Occasionally we drove past a bleak town – breeze-block constructions and concrete reinforced with rusted webs of iron' (2009: 35). Metcalfe skilfully constructs a torrid dystopia – a land of melancholy that globalization forgot. There is something awful about its sense of disconnection from the world, a disconnection that makes fashionable theories about globalization, digital networks and a knowledge economy seem like the excited ramblings of a privileged Western mind. How can we talk of 'globalization' when the world still features places like this, cut off and doomed to a fate of terminal decline and utter obscurity?

Amid the torrent of globalization writings it is easy to miss a significant literature that is sceptical about the whole notion of growing planetary connections and digital interconnectivity. This chapter will explore a large and diverse literature produced by a range of writers often grouped together as 'global sceptics'. They argue in various ways that globalization is mythological, inaccurate, worthless, hugely exaggerated or otherwise simply false as a concept. Global sceptics range from those who question the usefulness and accuracy of the term to those who come close to being globalization deniers. In various ways they attack the viewpoints of the globalization writers or the 'hyperglobalists' introduced in Chapter 1.

Debates about the newness, extent and impact of globalization are often shaped by differences of viewpoint across academic disciplines. For example, those trained to focus on the micro formations and meanings of local life (such as anthropologists, social historians, regional specialists and linguists) might be expected to be sceptical of a so-called 'globalization' that is ushering in total change and flux to all societies. Taking a microscopic rather than a helicopter focus, writers working in the traditions of ethnography or anthropology enter their communities and subcultures of interest and note down all kinds of behaviours and worldviews of these communities. Often using nothing more sophisticated than a pen and notepad, they go about recording the minutiae of behaviour, rituals and settings. From such a viewpoint, notions of global connections or a global society often seem remote, almost ludicrous. And yet, many ethnographers and anthropologists have made connections between the everyday and the global (Burawoy et al., 2000; see also Thompson, 2014: 7). There is a very interesting stream of highly detailed ethnographic literature on global industries, such as investment banking (Ho, 2009), arms trading (Nordstrom, 2004), or domestic cleaning services employing migrant women from less-developed countries (Parreñas, 2001). Such writings highlight the complex interplay of immediate and local forces with broader, perhaps less obviously visible, global forces that operate at a distance but affect local everyday life. Again, this shows the schizoid, unclear and to an extent contradictory nature of globalization writings.

At first glance, global scepticism appears absurd. How, when daily surrounded by evidence of increasingly intense global forces, structures, networks and risks, can anyone seriously suggest that globalization is a myth? This chapter will show, however, that the sceptical literature actually makes a lot of important points, and will argue that it is essential to consult and discuss it if we want to gain a rounded understanding of the contested processes and outcomes of globalization. The chapter is arranged in the following way. Firstly we will explore the arguments of those who regard the notion of 'globalization' as an historically naïve, faddish and rather superficial concept. We then go on to look at those who question the actual empirical existence of globalization, arguing that the excited claims of the globalization literature are exaggerated and that local features of social life remain much more significant than any putative global ones. We then explore the view that globalization is a weak, vague and contradictory idea that just cannot function properly as a theory or concept at all.

Before we begin it is important to note that the globalization *sceptics* are largely different from the globalization *critics* (although there are some points of connection). The critics *do* believe that globalization exists and that terminologies of global 'ages' and global 'networks' are sensible. They are critical of globalization's effects, whereas the global sceptics doubt or deny the validity of globalization either as a really-existing phenomenon itself or as a meaningful theoretical concept that can describe and explain the empirical world in its enormous complexity.

A very useful and detailed paper that unpacks the positions of the supporters, sceptics and critics of globalization was written by Mauro Guillén. He asks whether globalization is 'civilizing, destructive, or feeble' (Guillén, 2001). 'Feeble' would be a good word for the sceptics to use when they describe the veracity, value and relevance of globalization as a concept and a body of literature. It captures the sceptics' disdain for an idea they regard as intellectually unsound. There is much value in their position, but the chapter will not accept the sceptical view uncritically. Instead it will question the meaning and value of a sceptical position. To go back to that sorry city of Nukus for a moment, one might suggest that even here we see international connections of various kinds. Metcalfe's book often mentions young people desperate to leave the place, such as a law student who dreams of studying in America (Metcalfe, 2009: 33). Although most readers won't have heard of Karakalpakstan, they may well be aware of one of the reasons why the place is so economically depressed and the main reason Metcalfe (and Gill) visited. It is the site of the drastically shrunken Aral Sea, once a huge thriving inland sea that Soviet economic planners reduced to a parched and toxic wasteland in their efforts to irrigate nearby regions for export cotton production. The region is struggling so badly because of a mishandled attempt to forcibly integrate a part of this region's economy into the global economy in a narrow and reckless fashion. Global connections often exist in the strangest of places and can take on peculiar, non-linear forms. So it might be wrong to point to a depressed region and say: 'Where's your so-called "globalization" now?' To some extent, economic isolation can actually be related in certain ways to the very processes of globalization that the sceptics tend to deny or downplay. As this chapter will show, the sceptical literature struggles with its own limits and contradictions, just like the pro-globalist literature it attacks.

Various versions of global scepticism exist (Scholte, 2005: 18; Steger, 2005: 23). We begin our discussion by exploring the ideas of a range of authors who argue that globalization processes are nothing new. According to them globalization theory can't be taken seriously because it is ahistorical and exaggerated.

Historical scepticism: Globalization as nothing new

In *American Colonies*, the historian Alan Taylor provides a wonder-fully detailed account of the complexities and controversies of successive waves of European colonization of the 'New World', the American continent:

> The first European explorers were stunned by the distinctive flora, fauna, and human cultures found in the Americas. [...] But the differences began to diminish as soon as they were recognized. The invasion by European colonists, microbes, plants, and livestock eroded the biological and cultural distinctions formerly enforced by the Atlantic Ocean. Newly connected, the two 'worlds', old and new, became more alike in their natures, in their combinations of plants and animals. (Taylor, 2001: 24–5)

The above passage reads very much like a piece of 'globalization' writing; connections are taking place, cultures are clashing and merging, difference and distance are being destroyed. Yet Taylor is describing events that took place in the fifteenth and sixteenth centuries. Others have described the British East India Company (established in 1600) as the world's first multinational corporation (Robins, 2006). We are led to believe that globalization is a dramatic new development that emerged in the 1990s and remade the world anew. But the processes of European colonization and expansion date back over five hundred years. Does the notion of globalization make any sense in this context? Can it really be considered anything new?

Colonization of the Americas is just one very famous historical example of a long-term process involving human movement, exploration, technological development, trade and conquest. The so-called Silk Road is another. The term 'Silk Road' is something of a misnomer; the 'Road' was actually a web of trading routes across land, sea and river that stretched from Japan and Korea, through central and southern Asia, China, India, on to Samarkand in present-day Uzbekistan, Iran, through to Egypt, Byzantium and the fringes of Europe. Of course, a great many more commodities than silk were traded; paper travelled from China through the Islamic world and into parts of Europe in the eighth century, for example (Hansen, 2012). The heyday of the Silk Road was around 200 BCE to 1500 CE (Metcalfe, 2009: 4).

Long-distance trade, exploration, settlement and military conquest are consistent events in human history. Raw materials were imported into Early Mesopotamia in the third millennium BCE, and Babylonian and Indian societies had established trade routes from around 800 BCE (Held et al., 1999: 152). Could this mean that globalization is far from new but is rather a constant feature of human life since antiquity? When did globalization start? The settlement of North America by Europeans in the sixteenth century? What about Nordic settlements in Newfoundland in the tenth century? Or the 'native Americans', who were originally not indigenous to North America but rather travelled over centuries (45,000–12,000 BCE) across a land-bridge from what is now Siberia? Some claim that the world is 'one interacting whole and always has been' (McNeil, 2015: 148). Why, ask sceptics, did we start to use the word 'globalization' in the 1980s and 1990s when human movements, connections and empires were well-established many centuries earlier (Ferguson and Mansbach, 2012: 40–74; King, 2017: 1–7)?

This is a core argument of the global sceptics. Globalization is a buzzword or fad that naively fixates on present-day or very recent developments and mistakenly believes that the present is radically different from the past. Its main authors and proponents have become convinced by seductive but vacuous claims of radical breakages with history. The focus on the enabling power of new technologies and on the rapid growth in the power of multinational corporations distorts the historical reality of prior developments and the near-constant movements of people, technology, culture and wealth in history (and pre-history). How much has really changed since the 'global' era? Gender studies scholars have also objected to notions of radically new global eras or forces that transcend or escape the enduring importance of gendered social constructs such as family, marriage and domesticity (Acker, 2004; Gottfried, 2004).

One of the most famous sceptical pieces is Hirst and Thompson's (later Hirst, Thompson and Bromley's) *Globalization in Question*, a book that has run to three editions since the first was published in 1996. It is arguably the most detailed and advanced statement of the sceptical position and has been widely debated and cited. They don't go back especially far into human history to make their point that a globalizing or highly internationalized economy is nothing new. Their work includes no discursions through Mesopotamia or ancient China. Their discussion begins in the early nineteenth century and focuses in particular from the 1860s onwards, when processes of industrialization and the establishment of modern, urban societies started to really take root in Europe, North America and Japan. They claim that the internationalization of capitalism is nothing new (it has been ongoing on a very substantial basis since around the 1850s), and that in some ways previous eras in history actually exhibit stronger evidence of interconnectedness than today.

They note that international trade made up a larger percentage of many nations' GDP in 1913 than it did in 1995 (Hirst et al., 2009: 24–67). Hirst and colleagues particularly emphasize that nation states remain very significant actors whose power has not been eroded or destroyed by globalization. In fact, in certain ways national governments in the most advanced economies become even more central in their roles of setting the terms under which the global economy operates. Globalization is far from inevitable and unstoppable. Hirst et al.'s explanation of how the world economy has expanded and contracted at various times (the establishment and subsequent collapse of the Gold Standard, the 1929 Wall Street Crash and the Great Depression in the 1930s, the collapse of the Bretton Woods system of currency exchange in the early 1970s) dovetails with discussion about changes in policy discourses. Clearly national governments, political parties, bureaucrats and regulators were deeply involved in attempts to understand and influence the global economy at national and even international levels. Their efforts weren't irrelevant to the processes of globalization, suggesting that globalization is not some free-floating, unmanageable and irreversible new phenomenon, but is actually contributed to, encouraged by and sometimes restricted by government policy.

These are all important claims that add much-needed historical context, detail and realism to the often-excited globalization literature. Others have countered by suggesting that comparisons of the 2000s with the era of classical liberalism are spurious in that they ignore the quantum leaps in technology that have created a world economy qualitatively different from the industrial system of the nineteenth or early twentieth centuries. '[T]he biggest difference is in the level of finance and capital flows. Geared as it is to electronic money – money that exists only as digits in computers – the current world economy has no parallels in earlier times' (Giddens, 1999: 9).

I suppose it all depends on what one means by 'parallels'. If we are talking about international trade, technological change, migration and interconnectivity, then clearly there are meaningful historical parallels to be made between the present day and prior eras of industrial capitalism. Hirst et al., and other historically informed globalization scholars (Held et al., 1999; Osterhammel and Petersson, 2005), make a credible case that globalization as we know it today was forged in the white heat of the industrial revolution. Going further back into history and pre-history to show that humans have always migrated and traded over distance perhaps does not really help the global sceptical argument because the volume of world trade before the advent of modern industrial society was peripheral – only 1–2% of world economic activity (Held et al., 1999: 154). While humans have always migrated and in many cases shown ingenuity in developing the technological capacity to do so, the processes of interaction and movement were glacially slow in comparison to the explosion of activity since the industrial revolution that swept Europe and North America in the latter part of the nineteenth century.

Estimates of world GDP over time suggest general economic growth in much of the world's regions between the years 1 and 1870, then explosively rapid growth ever since. One estimate shows, for example, that the GDP of the region now known as Germany grew from $1,225 million in year 1 to $13,650 million in year 1700, then from $72,149 million in 1870 to $237,332 million in 1913 (Maddison, 2007: 379). That latter period of around 50 years saw revolutionary change in relation to the very slow development of the prior 15 to 20 centuries. Rutger Bregman, in *Utopia for Realists* argues that the last two centuries have seen 'stupendous' progress and that even 'those who we still call poor will enjoy an abundance unprecedented in world history' (Bregman, 2016: 13).

The industrial revolution provided the platform for the take-off phase of what later came to be called globalization. Twenty-five countries agreed in 1844 to set up three time zones and a concept of global time based on the Greenwich meridian, a system adopted almost everywhere by 1913 (Osterhammel and Petersson, 2005: 82–3). Electrical communication was pioneered around 1850 (McNeil, 2015: 144) and spread rapidly. Management and organizational ideas were also widely proliferated and adopted, especially towards the beginning of the First World War (Brech et al., 2010).

If steam power, electricity, shipping, railroads and heavy engineering were the hardware of international business, then cost accounting and statistical quality control were its software. The cultural circuits of consumer capitalism started to really establish themselves in the early twentieth century: department stores, advertising, merchandising, branding (Leach, 1993). A strong case can be made that 'globalization' starts with industrialism in the latter half of the nineteenth century; essentially the position that Hirst and colleagues advance. In doing so, it is vital to note that globalization was directed by elites and by governments – industrialization went hand in hand with colonization, empire-building, military force and the Atlantic slave trade (Cooke, 2003; Robins, 2006). It also made significant use of import tariffs and other forms of government support to national industry in ways that today would be considered grave and costly violations of free-market economic policies (Chang, 2003). Processes of globalization are contingent and to a significant extent planned and enforced, not something inevitable and uncontrollable or an outgrowth of 'natural' laws of markets and efficiency.

Like many fashionable ideas, the theory of a free-floating, inevitable, market and technology-driven globalization has taken on a life of its own, regardless of evidence to the contrary. Some of the sceptics' points are useful in providing a more historically informed and sober account of our supposedly radically new global economy. These authors are probably right to suggest that globalization is not a new phenomenon but can sensibly be traced back around 150 years. As the next section shows, other sceptics go beyond this and argue that globalization's contemporary extent is also highly contentious.

Empirical scepticism: Globalization as exaggeration

For the mainstream promoters of economic globalization we already live in a global age in which international markets, fuelled by digital and financial innovation, continue to connect humanity in ways that promote technological advancement, transnational cooperation and economic growth. For its (mostly) left-wing critics, the forces of globalization are also perceived to be extensive and growing. Supporters and critics both claim that a global economy and a global consciousness have developed rapidly in the last 50 years or so and they expect them to continue spreading to all corners of the globe. For supporters and critics, the real-world existence of globalization is axiomatic. Where they disagree is the social and moral value of these developments.

Sceptics argue, however, that globalization is by no means as advanced as its proponents and detractors claim. Is a global economy really a self-evident truth? According to sceptical analysis about the reality of international economy, the widely held view of an already intensely integrated global economy is 'simply wrong' (Ghemawat, 2011: 11). One of the most powerful sceptical arguments focuses on how a very large proportion of the world's population is cut off from so-called 'globalization'. The world economy – far from being truly global – is actually structured and defined by regional blocs. The vast majority of trade and investment takes place in and between essentially three regions: a 'triad' of Western Europe, North America and East and Southeast Asia (Dicken, 2007: 38–9; Pauly and Reich, 1997: 1–2). These are the core parts of the so-called 'global' economy, to which the rest of the world is, to varying degrees, peripheral (Dicken, 2007; Ghemawat 2009, 2011; Hirst et al., 2009: 73–6). The majority of *Fortune* magazine's annual Global 500 list of multinational corporations is headquartered in the USA, Japan, China, or Western Europe. Sheppard (2016: 17) cites research on international internet bandwidth that shows a mostly triangular pattern of USA/Canada–Europe–East Asia, with smaller branches to Latin America and (much less broadly) Africa.

Sutcliffe and Glyn (1999), in an article on measures of globalization in 1999, find all kinds of methodological problems in the ways in which globalization is accounted for. They claim to be 'still underwhelmed' by evidence that purports to show a dramatic new hyper-interactive global economy. A multivariate 'Global Index' developed by Raab et al. (2008) suggests a steady but very incomplete spread of political, economic, cultural and socio-technical globalization. Globalization processes have accelerated everywhere since the 1990s but there remains very distinct differences between regions categorized as 'global players' (Europe, Oceania and North America) and 'catching-up regions' (emerging economies in Asia, Latin America or the Caribbean). While still globalizing in absolute terms Africa seems to be doing so at a slower rate in relation to the others and might be falling further behind. African nations appear to be 'globalization laggards' (Raab et al., 2008). Ghemawat (2011) coins the term 'semiglobalization' to account for the partiality of these international connections.

It's probably safe to say that globalization is far from universal. It is actually a very uneven and contingent process. The internationalization of capitalism, technology or culture is always partial and incomplete, and so-called globalization actually depends on critical local features. Several authors have identified the importance of so-called 'global cities', such as Tokyo, London, or New York where vital financial organizations are located (Sassen, 2006; Golding, 2002. There are also several key industry clusters such as Silicon Valley in California (Barley and Kunda, 2004) or the 'industrial districts' of Northern Italy which are hotspots of cutting-edge small engineering and design companies (Rabellotti and Schmitz, 1999). Italian wines are certainly a global product but the information and expertise upon which its production depends is shared only between vital local points (Morrison and Rabellotti, 2009). Less glamorous examples can also be used in this line of argument, such as the indispensible role played by airport freight depots or shipping container ports in facilitating international trade and inward investment (Dicken, 2007: 430–1). Science parks, improved transit systems, new office space and hotels and free-trade zones are developed by local and national authorities in high-profile plays to attract global investment, such as the Skolkovo technology park in Moscow. Cities and regional authorities compete vigorously with each other to attract world freight through their hubs, global financial investments through their banks and elite white-collar expert workers to their top corporations and professions.

Even when business is genuinely transnational the practices and norms of business remain far from simple or harmonized. There have been many efforts to develop a more seamlessly integrated, globalized and standardized world society. But the outcomes of these efforts are mixed. A famous example is the language of Esperanto, originally created by Ludovic Zamenhov in the late nineteenth century in a remarkable attempt to develop a global, logically organized language free of cultural bias that could be spoken by all peoples of the world. It never really took off (Patterson and Huff, 1999). Product markets are often regionally diverse. Major automobile groups have failed several times in their attempts to develop a simple, cost-effective global car model that will sell in all regions of the world, yet car markets remain geographically distinct. Manufacturers often distinguish their product strategies by continent (Maxton and Wormald, 2004).

International industry standards differ widely. The medical world has, for example, laboured for decades to establish practical international standards for the collection and sharing of clinical information. There have been some successes, but the overall trend seems to be toward a cacophony of competing systems (Patterson and Huff, 1999). Even medical knowledge itself is contested and internationally differentiated, having its own cultural and historical path-dependence and reflecting different norms around what qualifies as knowledge or fact. In Japan, for example, depression has traditionally been thought of as primarily a physical rather than a mental ailment, implying no real Japanese market for antidepressant drugs developed by Western pharmaceutical companies (Harding, 2016). Various parts of the world have different industry standards for electrical voltage or weights and measurement and use variously shaped power sockets, railway gauges and systems of road traffic management. These differences can be overcome and worked around, of course. Huge efforts are expended on standardization and harmonization, as exemplified by the International Organization for Standards (ISO), a non-profit organization based in Switzerland to which over 160 national standards bodies are affiliated. It has developed tens of thousands of international standards such as the ISO 9000 series of quality standards. But the overall sceptical point holds. Standardization can be very hard to realize and the unintended consequences of its pursuit can be more harmful than the problem itself. How much would it cost to get rid of pint glasses or road signs marked in miles? In any case there wouldn't be any point; we can cope well enough without such standards and a so-called global economy functions reasonably adequately with wide variations in standards and practices.

A substantial academic literature discusses the huge range of customs and institutions that exists in the world economy. Yes, there is increasing internationalization in world business, and perhaps it is correct to call this 'globalization', but none of this means an increasing convergence in business practice. Germany, the United States, Japan, Russia, or China, for example, have all developed their own 'varieties of capitalism' or 'national business systems' that differ in many ways and to a large extent endure despite globalization (Dore, 2000; McCann, 2014a). International joint ventures and foreign direct investment projects often break down amid international rows about strategy, taxation or repatriation of profits, or founder on the rocks of cultural misunderstandings or clashing legal rulings. Working overseas is difficult. A large literature in the field of international management discusses the enduring problem of 'expatriation failure rates' where business executives find it impossible to work effectively in unfamiliar overseas surroundings.

Just like the different shapes and sizes of power sockets or railway gauges, idiosyncratic national institutions and 'ways of doing business' persist and survive. The world economy seems to tolerate these differences and the parallel ways in which national business systems operate. Perhaps the global economy doesn't need to converge, and the assumptions about the inevitability of convergence or adoption of global 'standards' reflect a Western arrogance about the superiority of their systems. For all the global talk, economics is dominated by local activity. Ghemawat (2009: 56) estimates that around 90% of phone calls, web traffic and investment is local rather than transnational.

Much globalization theory speculates about the decline of nation states and the rise of a borderless world. But, related closely to arguments above about the importance and persistence of national institutions, global sceptics argue that nation states that have been powerful since the industrial revolution remain highly influential in structuring the world economic order (Hirst et al., 2009; Weiss, 1998). These nations' interests are most heavily represented in transnational political organizations such as the UN or the World Bank. Moreover, when it suits them, the most powerful nation states can skirt around or ignore these bodies (Martell, 2007: 175). China and Russia have recently re-emerged as major world powers exerting their political, geo-strategic and economic interests, backed by their increasingly globally prominent state media broadcasters such as Russia Today or CCTV. With long histories of communism and political authoritarianism neither is shy about exerting state control over some parts of their economies such as banking, telecommunications, heavy industry and military applications. Many claim that the Chinese state continues to play a vital role in the growth of its economy (Naughton, 2007). Major Chinese investments into Africa are increasingly notable and none of this takes place without the direct involvement of Chinese government officials (Carmody, 2011).

In relation to state power, there is arguably no real threat in sight to the principle whereby nations (broadly) respect the national sovereignty and territorial integrity of others. This dates back to the Treaty of Westphalia in 1648. National governments are elected only by national citizens and their daily reliance on bureaucracy, legal systems and established procedures shows how power, authority and governance are embedded deeply into local structures that usually date back generations. For all the talk of international connections, a global village or a global culture, significant power still resides at local levels (Thompson, 2014). This power is made manifest when a person enters a court room, is pulled over by a police officer or applies for a visa. Centuries of laws and regulations are enacted in the special powers possessed by those in official positions and represented in the badges or robes of office of police officers or judges. The judiciary is often the final arbiter of disputes and claims at many levels of society. The power of government is further demonstrated every day in professional routines and bureaucratic forms and procedures. This idea is Foucauldian in some sense, but also Marxian and Weberian; ultimately government power is based on its license to use force and/or its threat. Max Weber famously wrote in

1919 of the state's monopoly over the use of violence. Lenin repeatedly mentions 'special bodies of armed men' in *The State and Revolution* (1917). The genealogy of this thinking can be seen in classical works of political philosophy and law such as Hobbes' *Leviathan* (1651) or Bodin's *Les Six Livres de la République* (1576). It would take a truly dramatic change for 'globalization' to somehow overturn the ways in which sovereign power is manifested and legitimized over centuries of human existence.

Of course, globalization is associated with the growth of transnational legal frameworks such as European law, or the regulations and structures of transnational treaties such as CETA. But, contrary to populist views about excessive EU bureaucracy or conspiratorial rants about 'world government', these structures have not replaced national sovereignty. Rather they sit alongside them in complex relationships. Centuries of legal structures, precedents and judgements at the national level remain by far the most important influence on juridical authority (Lindahl, 2013).

Pro-globalists will suggest that globalization involves efforts to get around national restrictions or to find ways to harmonize them at international or 'supraterritorial' levels (Scholte, 2005). But, ironically, efforts to do this sometimes mean the amplification of local influences. For example, the US government's use of military detention centres at Guantanamo Bay Naval Base for the holding and interrogating of 'enemy combatants' was clearly related to a desire to avoid the Geneva Conventions that apply to the treatment of prisoners of war. This evasive and abusive behaviour created international outrage and brought the hidden 'non-place' of Guantanamo to the world's attention. A similar dynamic means that tiny and otherwise obscure territories such as the Cayman Islands, British Virgin Islands or Turks and Caicos have become notorious as secretive tax havens which enable 'aggressive tax planning' (Fichtner, 2014). Physical location remains centrally important in a globalized world even when the operations of a globalizing party aim to be placeless and traceless.

This relates to another important sceptical argument surrounding the nature of the world economy – its physical, corporeal nature. Globalization literature tends to imagine the world economy as weightless, fluid and digitized – a world economy of ideas, finance, information, culture and knowledge that moves effortlessly through fibre-optic cables and across Wi-Fi networks (Bauman, 2000; Castells, 2000). Yet the global, digital, offshored economy has to materialize at certain physical points (Rainnie et al., 2008). Sceptics will argue that the 'knowledge economy' is exaggerated and that mundane and 'heavy' items are absolutely crucial elements of international business, such as fossil fuels, container ships, electricity generation, electronic cabling or steel manufacturing. Oil and oil-derived products remain central to the functioning of the world economy. Yes, there is a global economy of sorts, but it rests on vital local architectures that enable, regulate and police international transactions. These range from physical and technological artefacts, to geographic and regulatory loopholes, to the 'fixers' who informally regulate legal, semi-legal and illegal trades (Nordstrom, 2007). Without access to trusted local knowledge and connections, many forms of international trade – major or small-scale – cannot happen. Hidden and questionable practices are abundant at many levels of global and local economic activity, ranging from outright bribery and racketeering to other forms of corrupt and semi-corrupt practices, such as corporate lobbying and the use of middlemen (Feldman, 2013; Granter, 2017).

Multinational corporations market themselves as genuinely global corporations with no enduring ties to any one nation. They often downplay their historical roots by rebranding the company to remove specific country references. But sceptical literature on multinationals has tended to emphasize the widely overlooked importance of locality. Rather than being genuinely global, multinationals would be more accurately understood as domestic firms with overseas units that are managed quite tightly from the centre. The HQ is a corporation's centre of gravity. Boards of directors of large MNCs are usually dominated by home-country nationals (Doremus et al., 1999; Pauly and Reich, 1997). They are likely to think and act in similar ways, to promote executives with similar personal backgrounds up the corporate hierarchy, to put the interests of domestic stakeholders first, and to repatriate significant profits back to the country of origin. They frequently set up, benefit from and maintain distinctly locally bound structures such as industrial cartels. Their top executives are densely networked into national governments and agencies.

Globalization writings have a difficult time unravelling the relationships of 'global' to 'local'. The language of globalization strains and contorts as authors try to reconcile these positions, resulting in the development of strange portmanteau terms such as 'glocalization'. This term, often associated with the work of Roland Robertson (Ritzer, 2010: 255), seems to be a translation of a Japanese word *dochakuka* meaning 'global localization' (Robertson, 1992: 173–4; 1994). The idea appears to have been promoted by the Sony Corporation in describing its product strategy (Dicken, 2007: 138–9). But it's difficult to get a real handle on what it means in practice. An interesting paper on South Korea's globalization (Park et al., 2007) suggests the existence of both strong 'localness' and strong 'globalness'.

Korea retains powerful social norms of nationalism yet also is highly globally dependent and in some ways subservient to Western-led transnational organizations as shown in the IMF bailout following the 1997 Asian financial crash. While it seems plausible for local and global to be thought of as simultaneously powerful forces, we introduce a real lack of clarity into our analysis if terms such as 'global' and 'local' are conveniently merged. Globalization literature wanders between different levels of abstraction and often cannot plausibly explain the underlying dynamics. 'Glocalization' would be a particular manifestation of this problem. Personally, I've always disliked this ugly term as I think it sums up the meaninglessness and circularity of so much of the globalization literature. I can see what it refers to: the awkward and complex coexistence of local and global features. But '-ization' suggests a process, action or result of some kind. What are these movements or transformations? Where and how do they take place? By what means can something be glocalized? Can a person, product or a place be glocalized? And by whom? Can something be de-glocalized? This is starting to sound like gibberish.

Globalization is 'a word that overuse has made so elastic, it has almost lost definition' (Perry, 2008: 18). The turn towards 'globalizations' in the plural reflects this deep struggle for meaning. Sceptics believe the term is so imprecise that it is basically unworkable as any kind of serious academic theory. It is perhaps more sensible to speak of globalization as an area of study or an umbrella term under which all manner of further concepts and processes take place. Globalization as plural; globalizations with an 's'. But if that's the best we can do to rescue the concept then what is the point? A third area of global sceptical literature argues that globalization is a junk concept, dumbed-down and worthless, or is perhaps part of a broader corporate ideology that should be rejected. We will now explore these particular ideas in more depth as we bring this chapter towards its conclusion.

Conceptual scepticism: Globalization as an unworkable theory

A final sceptical view regards globalization theory as simplistic and naïve. From this viewpoint, globalization is a corporate, academic and journalistic hype product. Susan Strange once complained that the notion is used to refer to 'anything from the internet to a hamburger' (Strange, 1996: xii–xiii; see also Steger, 2005: 23–7). Globalization as a concept is so vague, contradictory and all-encompassing that it cannot rightly be considered a theory at all, certainly not in the sense of classic social science ideas as 'rationalization', 'alienation' or 'industrialization'. Instead, globalization is an indistinct buzzword that refers only to a much more general series of uneven processes. At best, it just about works as an umbrella term for a broad field of study in which many other ideas reside.

In his books *Selling Globalization* and *Globaloney 2.0*, Michael Veseth argues that globalization is simply a powerfully told and regularly repeated story circulated by international elites. He argues that it 'hardly matters whether the story is true or false. What matters is that people accept the story and use it to justify a set of actions and to further a set of interests' (Veseth, 2010: 32). We've certainly seen this many times in the rhetoric of politicians, such as blaming poverty and joblessness on 'the forces of globalization' thus conveniently shifting blame away from governments' own national policies. Veseth argues that globalization is a trope rather than a workable theory, and his texts include all manner of examples of globalization as an exaggerated and mythological idea that constrains the imagination of other possibilities. The title of the latter book is a reference to US Congresswoman Clare Boothe Luce of Connecticut describing Secretary of Commerce Henry Wallace's proposed 'free skies' programme in 1944 as 'globaloney' (Veseth, 2010: 27). Here is an early example of right-wing opposition to globalization, in which Luce proposes putting American interests before any purported 'global' ones (see also Scholte, 2005: 15). Veseth suggests that the political Right and Left both exaggerate the benefits and dangers of globalization by making it mean almost anything with their excited rhetoric. 'Globalization can apparently destroy democracy, create it, and be used by political entrepreneurs to manipulate democracy. This globalization must be a terrible, wonderful thing' (Veseth, 1998: 12).

In describing globalization as hype, Veseth is not actually denying the existence of globalization in certain ways. Many other sceptics also agree that the current world economy is indeed highly internationalized (Hirst et al., 2009: 3). Thompson notes that his scepticism is 'milder' today compared to his writings with Hirst in the 1990s (2014: 4). Sceptics such as Thompson, Hirst and Veseth do not actually deny globalization. Rather, they argue that the statements, imagery and language of globalization run some way ahead of the reality, creating unhelpful rhetorical distortions that have been widely accepted uncritically. Mainstream notions of unstoppable globalization are inaccurate because people believe the myth that nothing can be done to influence it. Veseth points to a number of prominent alter-globalization or anti-globalization movements such as the 'Slow Food' movement that emerged in Italy, or the hostility of much of French society to US-led globalization. While Veseth argues that global talk is often baloney, he also says globalization does exist and should be reformed to make it more humane and less oppressive. But in making this move Veseth's supposedly sceptical position becomes very similar to 'justice globalizers' such as Held and others who promote 'global civil society' and are often positioned in the hyperglobalist camp (Thompson, 2014: 9–10). Like a lot of the globalization literature that he criticizes, Veseth's own work is often contradictory, rhetorical and highly journalistic. We have returned to the idea that globalization is so large a field as to be inescapable; the sceptics use similar rhetorical tactics to those of the hyperglobalists in order to try to convince us that globalization is mythological. Ultimately the sceptics are unable to escape the circularity, superficiality and self-referential tropes of the globalization literature that they themselves criticize. As regards the Slow Food movement: '[t]he revolution began in Rome … at a McDonald's' (Veseth, 2010: 141).

Veseth's books are playful and ironic and he is too canny a writer to subscribe to some kind of 'all-out' globalization rejectionism. But the result is a half-scepticism to go with Ghemawat's 'semiglobalization'. In both the globalist and the sceptical literature we see endless provisos and qualifications. Very little is clear or unproblematic. To be fair to the globalization literature many other concepts in social science and humanities are also contentious and hard to define, such as art, culture, family, gender, power or history. It would not be fair to dismiss the concept of globalization as faddish and useless purely on the basis that the term itself is slippery and difficult to define.

Another sceptical position is to regard globalization theory as the ideology of corporate capitalism. This view suggests globalization is simply a new word for imperialism, Westernization, or Americanization, arguing that the internationalization of trade, investment, and product markets works in the favour of the core richest nations, exploiting the periphery of low-income countries that cannot fight back or put forward their own interests (Freeman and Kagarlitsky, 2004; Hardt and Negri, 2000). This is not so much global scepticism; rather it is re-characterizing globalization as imperialism. Anthropologist David Vine in *Base Nation* (2015) describes the US military's version of globalization whereby the world is divided into giant regional Commands such as USAFRICACOM, USCENTCOM, USSTRATCOM. Large chunks of the world are overseen by a career military officer known as a Unified Combatant Commander who almost acts as a regional plenipotentiary aiming to project American power (Johnson, 2006). The ideology of free-floating, networked, supraterritorial globalization diverts attention from much less palatable imaginations of what globalization can mean.

The arguments of global sceptics and global critics can start to merge when both draw attention to globalization as ideology that masks an uglier reality. A common device in the globalization literature is to talk of 'waves' of writings, starting with a first wave of hyperglobalist writings (see Chapter 1), moving to a second wave of sceptics and then on to some kind of third-wave synthesis in what is often called the 'transformationalist' position (see for example Hay and Marsh, 2000; Held et al., 1999). Third-wave globalization writers essentially reaffirm the existence of globalization but do so in a more detailed and less hysterical fashion than the early hyperglobalist literature. But in an interesting critique of the notion of 'waves' of globalization writings, sociologist Luke Martell (2007) suggests that there isn't much to choose between the sceptical and transformationalist position. Instead, the transformationalists actually sound a lot like the sceptics in describing a contingent and partial international arena in which certain nation states remain very powerful players. None of the sceptics are actually globalization deniers. They don't say that nothing has changed. It is more that they are uncomfortable with the talk of a globalized era that they see as exaggerated and unrealistic (Martell, 2007: 182). Sceptics or second wavers are less optimistic about the effectiveness of the kinds of global social movements that transformationalists are keen to emphasize. Instead, sceptics (like the critics we will encounter in Chapter 3) tend to see globalization as a power game in which the major players are likely to continue to hold on to their dominant positions. Martell writes:

> If transformationalists are basing normative globalist proposals on an analysis that shares common ground with that of the skeptics – that is, a world with unevenness in integration, stratification, reconstituted but active nation-states, re-territorialization, and regional blocs – then the pursuit of a cosmopolitan global democracy that they argue for becomes unlikely. (Martell, 2007: 194)

Sceptics tend to reinforce more traditional ways of understanding the world; not in terms of global networks and flows, cosmpolitian civil society, or supraterritoriality, but in terms of long-established corporate and political structures that retain enormous influence, such as the World Trade Organization, Royal Dutch Shell, the Chinese Communist Party, the IMF, or the US military.

Whether we or not approve of the word 'globalization', it has become an important idea that deserves discussion. It can capture the imagination and it does refer to something recognizable. Scholars such as Hay and Marsh (2000), Held et al. (1999), Hirst et al. (2009), Jessop (2000), Sheppard (2016), and Weiss (1998) have all produced very reasonable and scholarly accounts of globalization as an outcome or a set of processes, showing that globalization writings do not have to be simplistic or dumbed-down. Globalization can be described in detailed ways and its extent and limits can be carefully accounted for.

But, such is its looseness and lack of precision, globalization fares much less well if conceptualized as a distinct process or theory with explanatory power of its own. Some of the heavyweights of global studies (Giddens, Scholte and others) have been subjected to fierce criticism for what some see as imprecision and sophistry in their writings (the most angry example probably being Rosenberg, 2000). There is a danger of the concept trying to explain everything: globalization creates wealth and poverty, democracy and authoritarianism, convergence and divergence, war and peace, inclusion and exclusion (Thompson, 2014: 2). If globalization means everything then it effectively means nothing. That is probably a good enough reason in itself to be sceptical about the notion of globalization, or of globalization writings where the complexities of the world are reduced to some abstract process called 'globalization' with explanatory effects. Such a reductionist view is not very convincing and does a disservice to the multiple complexities and contingencies of international economic, political and cultural connections that have already been very well described and explained by a range of more traditional concepts. Rosenberg (2000: 165) claims that globalization theory is '[h]amstrung at a deeper, definitional level, [...] unable even to rise to a coherent propositional statement without incurring the charge of a category error.'

The sceptics generally make a convincing case to abandon globalization as a distinct academic theory with explanatory power. But in terms of something like 'globalization' actually existing, as understood in terms of steadily growing international connections enabled by technological, cultural, organizational and political changes (even if far from uniform in extent and reversible at times), then, yes, this thing called globalization does exist. Given the apparent acceleration and proliferation of these processes and outcomes since the 1970s, it also seems likely that globalization will continue to grow in influence.

The globalization sceptics usefully inform us that globalization has very uneven geographic impacts and is not radically new; its existence can be traced back to the industrial revolution. The sceptical literature has performed a valuable role in questioning the excesses of hyperglobalist arguments that can be naïve, distorting and disempowering. Globalization is often presented as inevitable, irreversible and largely unmanageable. But the sceptics – in showing that globalization is not especially new, is less extensive than is often thought, and not inevitable or unstoppable – suggest that there are alternatives to globalism and neoliberalism. It is around this area of thinking where global scepticism merges to some degree with the sensibilities of the globalization critics. We explore the arguments of the globalization critics in the following chapter.

3

Critics of Globalization in the North and South

They took our jobs!

(Cartoon American blue-collar workers in the US comedy TV
series *South Park*, 2004)

It was such a brilliant idea. And like many so many great ideas one wonders why no-one seems to have thought of it before. Episode 7 of the 8th season of *South Park* is entitled *Goobacks*. It tells the story of some peculiar characters which suddenly arrive one by one in an unremarkable American town. They are *time migrants*. Years in the future all jobs have been eliminated by automation and outsourcing, so these folk have travelled back in time from 3045 to the early 2000s to find work. The new arrivals are a pleasant curiosity at first. But when they start to arrive in larger numbers the good folk of South Park turn xenophobic and defensive. The migrants start to be pejoratively labelled 'goobacks' as, when regressing through time, some kind of strange ectoplasm glues up their bodies. The migrants undercut the labour market and willingly do the work of South Park labourers for a fraction of their wages, triggering layoffs and widespread unemployment. Right-wing TV covers the story with a formulaic face-off between 'pissed-off white trash redneck conservative' (the union boss attacking the migrants) and 'ageing liberal hippie douche' (some kind of NGO leader or academic defending them). The local construction workers' union has no real way of responding, getting ever more desperate and parochial in its reaction to the unwanted newcomers. They are unable to comprehend that the local work is not exclusively reserved for 'present time' people. '*They took our jobs!*' is all they can say by means of analysis. Over time they seem to lose the power of speech entirely.

What they eventually decide to do in their campaign to respond to the job-loss threat is too puerile and offensive to describe here, but is perhaps a comment on how workers (in particular men employed in blue-collar occupations with few qualifications) are vulnerable to global change and have so little recourse when matters turn against them. The union, far from being a progressive force struggling to raise the wages and status of working people, is totally outmanoeuvred and has become deeply conservative.

While obviously a comedy, this *South Park* episode makes some powerful points about globalization as tragedy. Insecurity, downward mobility and feelings of helplessness and disenfranchisement are endemic across many regions of the world, despite mainstream market globalizers such as Bhagwati or Wolf who insist that the expansion of economic globalization is in the interests of all. A large academic literature documents the damage done by global market forces to those who have 'lost out' to globalization. The controversies and challenges of migration, job loss and 'social dumping' (employers using labour forces that are cheaper than those previously available), are seemingly intensified by globalization, as global market forces hand more and more power to 'footloose' multinational corporations and make working people's lives ever more precarious.

A great deal of the literature that is critical of market globalism focuses on the impoverishment, rampant corruption, instability and war that blight the less-developed nations, 'the global South' – problems that are not helped by or are possibly worsened by new global interconnections. But 'the global North' (the economically most advanced world) is also deeply threatened by globalization. Sociologists Robert and Carolyn Perrucci sum up globalization's effects on American workers as 'a dagger thrust into the heart of hope' (Perrucci and Perrucci, 2008: 29), referring to factory closures, pay freezes, the destruction of pension funds and the collapse of unions, all brought home by globalization and met by indifference and inaction from those meant to represent local people such as political parties, unions and national governments. The same situation pertains to workers across the 'most-developed' countries. Critics of market globalization are today strongly emanating from the conservative Right, in some ways sharing the traditional Left's concern about the insecurity wrought by incessant market forces. Donald Trump repeatedly appealed to working class blue-collar voters in his successful 2016 Presidential election campaign in putting 'America First' and pledging to defend jobs from the global market threats represented by mass immigration, outsourcing and free trade agreements. Many commentators also saw the UK's June 2016 vote to exit the European Union as a vote against globalization and a rejection of the technocratic global, political and corporate elites that have lost touch with the realities of ordinary life. Critics of globalization make strange bedfellows as the forces of global change become ever more unpredictable and disturbing.

This chapter will explore the arguments put forward by a wide range of authors who are critical of the real-world effects that globalization has on much of the world's population. Rather than the sceptics of Chapter 2 who believe that globalization is exaggerated or mythological, the critics of this Chapter 3 insist that globalization is a set of powerful, really existing forces creating new problems for world society, such as new forms of worker exploitation by global corporations; the lack of governmental oversight and regulation of an increasingly risky and turbulent world economy; and rapid and severe growth in the levels of income inequality between the massed ranks of ordinary people and an increasingly remote new global elite (Klein, 2017). There are many ways in which globalization can be criticized, but this chapter focuses mostly on economic globalization or market globalism. Critics of free-market globalization are often labelled 'anti-globalization' but they might be more precisely defined as part of a broader 'alter-globalization' movement; they are not necessarily against the notion of a global society and many would not want to be considered xenophobic or nationalist. But they certainly are opposed to global market capitalism as summed up in their phrase 'another world is possible.'

We start by exploring the effects of globalization on the global South, the region often portrayed to be continually on the receiving end of globalization's harshest effects. We then move on to explore the arguments made by globalization critics about its baleful effects in the global North as traditional communities such as 'South Park, Colorado' get torn to shreds.

Grievances in the global South

Globalization is a set of modernizing processes that compress time and space, bringing all parts of the world into closer contact. In the economic realm we have become accustomed to thinking of a global economy or world market forces, to such a degree that almost every element of economic activity is interconnected and interdependent. Global corporate brands, such as Nike, Coca-Cola, Toyota, Siemens and Samsung are highly visible and recognized across practically the entire world. To its proponents and defenders our new global economy increases economic efficiency and draws all regions of the world into mutually beneficial economic expansion and development. Globalization, through free trade and instant communication, is spreading the benefits of wealth, technology and democracy.

But we know from Chapter 2 of this book that much of the world remains isolated from these supposedly beneficial global trade links. In a speech peppered with fashionable 'global governance' rhetoric in the immediate aftermath of the 9/11 attacks, UK Prime Minister Tony Blair described the condition of Africa as 'a scar on the conscience of the world' that needs addressing by the increased economic integration of some of the poverty-stricken, war-torn African nations (Blair, 2001). The implication is that globalization can and will assist in the economic and political development of these countries if more time and effort is expended in that direction. Given time, global trade and investment will surely assist in the development of these neglected regions, which historically had been brutally exploited by powerful European nations during colonial times.

But critics of globalization are scornful of the idea that globalization will eventually improve the condition of less-developed nations. Instead they claim that, through increased interconnectivity, globalization in many ways actively creates and sustains poverty. Globalization provides the governments, corporations and transnational organizations of the rich 'global North' with new ways of continuing to exploit the 'global South'. The North has no genuine interest in the development of the South (Chang, 2003; Reinert, 2007). As ever, it is only interested in what it can get for itself, just like the hateful and repressive colonial system of the past (Badiou, 2016: 24–30). It is certainly true that regions in sub-Saharan Africa, central and southern America and South Asia are much weaker economically than those of Western Europe and North America (Ferguson, 2006: 1–23; Glennie, 2008). But is this underdevelopment due to the *lack* of global connections as a mainstream globalizer such as Tony Blair would argue? Or are the grotesque inequalities between developing and developed nations actually *sustained and reproduced by global trade*? Critics of globalization would generally argue the latter. We will explore their views in this section.

The global South is defined and classified in all kinds of contentious ways. The World Bank has five classifications of groups of nations by their Gross National Income per capita: Low Income ($1,025 or less per capita per year), Lower-Middle Income ($1,026–$4,035), Upper-Middle Income ($4,036–$12,475), and High Income ($12,476 and above). At the time of writing (2016) the low-income group comprised around 31 countries, the lower-middle 52, the upper-middle 55, and the high income 79. Thirty-one is the lowest number of countries ever recorded in the bottom bracket, having shrunk from 64 in 1994. The sum total of the population living in low-income countries has fallen from 3.1 billion in 1994 to 613 million in 2014 (Anderson, 2015) with the world's total population at around 7.4 billion. Poverty, disease, malnutrition and lack of education have declined significantly in the last ten years (Bregman, 2016: 13–19). A powerful case can be made that globalization is in fact reducing misery quite rapidly and that what the populations of the developing world want is more globalization, not less. Developing countries want to emulate the high-income countries and eventually reach their status and the only way to do this is to wholeheartedly enter the global economic system and its neoliberal rules of free trade and open borders (Bhagwati, 2007; Wolf, 2004).

But how long is the developing world supposed to wait for their wealth to increase? Clearly there remains a deep chasm between the global wealthy and the global poor. According to the UN's World Food Programme, nearly 800 million people in the world have insufficient food to live a healthy life. That's more than 10% of the world's population. Chronic hunger is almost exclusively a developing-world problem; 779 million of those suffering food shortages live in developing regions and 14.7 million in the developed world. About 20% of the African population faces food insecurity, around 12% of Asia, 5.5% of Latin America and 14% of Oceania. Less than 5% of the population of the developed world faces this appalling problem (Food and Agriculture Organization of the United Nations, 2015: 8). Research by the polling organization Pew claimed that around 70% of the world's population lives on ten dollars or less per day (Kochhar, 2015b). For all the headlines about reductions in the basest levels of poverty, the vast majority of the world's population remains clustered in the lower income brackets: 15% are classified 'poor' and 56% 'low income' on Pew's methodology. Only 7% enjoy 'high' incomes of $50 or more per day (Kochhar, 2015a). Critics will also claim that the poverty definition thresholds are all set too low.

I'll return to the issue of inequality later in the chapter. It's enough to say for now that the global poor are definitely still with us. Classic Leftist or Marxist literature on the world economy featured chronic poverty as a central issue, such as 'World-Systems' theory or 'dependency theory' in which a cosmopolitan core of rich countries dominates and exploits the periphery and semi-periphery (Ray, 2007: 21–4; Wallerstein, 2004). Peripheral countries house the majority of the world's population but very little of its wealth because their economies are trapped into unequal trade relations with the rich core. Less-developed nations are dependent on exports of low-value-added goods; typically commodities, such as minerals, bananas and cocoa for example, where margins are extremely low and where competition takes place on cost rather than added-value such as scientific innovation (Reinert, 2007). Unlike the richest nations of the world these countries have failed to industrialize and to develop expertise in high-value-added goods and services. In a global economy, these markets are almost the exclusive preserve of nations from a 'triad' of Western Europe, North America and East Asia (Dicken, 2007: 39). Oxford economist Paul Collier writes of a 'bottom billion'; a group of countries with a combined population of around a billion people that seems perhaps permanently 'trapped' by political, economic and geographic constraints. Globalization might be leading to integration and growth for much of the developing world but it does nothing for these nations. Foreign aid and international trade appear unhelpful because the political-economic structures of these societies are so dysfunctional that aid, loans, free trade and inward investment serves only to sustain corrupt power structures of criminal gangs and venal governments. Daily life in these unfortunate places can be a harrowing experience of poverty and violence. If globalization makes the world 'flat' then these nations have 'fallen off the edge' (Perry, 2008).

But doesn't globalization bring new investments in technology, skills and jobs to the global South? Well, it does in part. But even this is contested by the critics. The alter-globalization journalist and campaigner Naomi Klein has made a particularly strong contribution to critical globalization literature. Her highly successful book *No Logo* (2010) was iconic, widely described as a 'bible' of the anti-globalization movement. It was first published just as the anti-globalization movement sprang to prominence with the anti-WTO protests in Seattle in 1999. She powerfully describes the ways in which globalization has transformed the prospects of growth and wealth-generation for already rich segments of global society while suppressing opportunities for the less fortunate. A central part of her argument is that recent developments in transnational communications and marketing have placed overwhelming importance on the role of corporate brands, visions and images, to the extent that global corporations such as Nike or Adidas concern themselves almost exclusively with their globalized, highly portable brands and can neglect the local, immobile production units that manufacture the actual physical items that bear the brands. To use Bauman's phraseology, brands are liquid whereas factories are solid, and it is the solid parts of a society that are increasingly 'melted down' by global forces. Production units are relocated from the global North to the global South to take advantage of cheap wages, tax breaks and weak environmental and labour standards. Production quotas set by the parent company are met by a network of outsourced sweatshops who exploit their vulnerable workers in ways described in horrible detail by Klein: very long shifts without meal or toilet breaks, poor safety standards, bullying management style, intimidation of anyone who even thinks of union organizing. There are rules against talking or even smiling at work (Klein, 2010: 211). Export Processing Zones are portrayed more like prisons than workplaces. The workforces are young, predominantly female, and have travelled long distances from rural regions, requiring the use of company dormitories. In one such location in Sri Lanka, Klein writes of workers sleeping on concrete floors, their spaces marked in white paint 'like car parks' (2010: 209). Horror stories reported by Klein are replicated today. For example, an appalling incident took place in 2013 when the eight-storey

Rana Plaza commercial complex in Dhaka, Bangladesh collapsed, crushing and trapping thousands of garment workers contracted to cheap clothing retailers in the West. Over a thousand workers were killed.

With the brand as king, huge mark-ups can be applied to the products of sweatshop labour such as iPhones or Nike clothing. Remote and complex chains of highly competitive subcontracting shields the parent company and creates plausible deniability; head office can claim it doesn't know about, encourage or condone the use of sweatshop labour. But the outsourced sweatshop remains a brutal secret lurking behind the funky countercultural brand discourses of companies such as Apple or Nike. Brand value speaks to the weightlessness and liquidity of the globalized economy, but someone somewhere has to stitch the clothes together or install electronic components at less than a dollar per hour. Workers in these 'discarded factories' (Klein, 2010: 195–229) don't get to 'Think different'; it's more a case of 'JUST DO IT'.

Again, however, the ideologists of market globalism will dispute such a critical view, claiming that low-paid jobs are substantially better than the alternative of no jobs, subsistence farming or criminal activities. By that reasoning globalization is therefore improving the objective conditions of working people in developing nations. If the pay and conditions at subcontractors for Apple and Sony are so bad then why have they got hundreds of young people queuing up at their gates asking for work each day? Maybe the conditions are tough, but they will improve – industrial work in the North also used to be dangerous, poorly paid and exploitative.

Globalization critics will respond to this line of argument by pointing to the huge profits generated by multinationals and suggest that much more could be done to improve pay, conditions and safety standards. Global trade can create new jobs in the developing world, but much of this work is clearly miserable and insecure. Do the multinationals really need to extract quite this much surplus from their production arrangements? Do they really have to immiserate their workers to such an extreme degree? How much profit is enough? What is a fair wage? Can we put a price on human dignity? Global market ideology, framed as it is solely in terms of aggregate estimations of wealth and profit, has little motivation or capacity to answer questions like these (Badiou, 2016).

Grievances in the global North

Given these severe problems in the global South one might imagine that living in the global North is easy. Comparatively, of course, this is true. As we've seen, the high-income countries have far higher wealth per capita, better access to vital services such as education and health-care, and (broadly) enjoy free media and functioning democratic systems as compared to low- and medium-income countries. But to say this is again to make very large-scale, aggregate comparisons. At the level of specific communities or individuals, the risks and dangers of globalization for those living in the richest OECD countries are often keenly felt. The global North is far from a utopian realm for many of its inhabitants.

Many ordinary people see their prospects for making a decent living threatened by globalization. Since the 1980s and the take-off of neolib-eralism, large segments of OECD labour forces have been increasingly vulnerable to job loss, job insecurity and work intensification. The opening of countries to globalization such as Mexico, India, China and the former USSR in the 1990s has brought potentially billions of people into a global labour market to compete for work, putting downward pressure on wages in the North. Migrants looking to find work in richer nations might be attractive to employers as they could be expected to accept lower wages and worse conditions than those currently employed. It is not just the movement of people into richer countries that can be a concern for workers. Jobs can also be exported outwards. As Klein explains, low-wage and low-tax zones set up in developing countries can attract employers looking to relocate work overseas in order to cut production costs and make savings on the entitlements granted to workers during the post-war years. The actual relocation of work clearly causes job loss. But the new abilities that globalization creates to *plausibly threaten* job loss has also grown, giving employers leverage over their work force: 'Improve your productivity or we'll move the jobs to China'; 'Your pension plan is now too costly, so we're getting rid of it'; 'Your quality and output numbers are lower here in Coventry than they are in the sister plant in Guangdong – shape up or we'll close you down'.

Employers' attacks on wages, pensions and job security have been well documented since the 1980s. Barry Bluestone and Bennett Harrison (1982) wrote of the *Deindustrialization of America* back in the early 1980s, the very beginning of President Ronald Reagan's neo-liberal revolution in the US. After 30 years of post-war economic growth and general job stability, suddenly industrial capacity and industrial jobs were put at risk because of the expansion of global com-petition that broke the relationship between employment and the local communities in which it is housed. Workers have ever-fewer means to control their own life chances. This dynamic is explored in microcosm in *Mollie's Job* (Adler, 2000), a book documenting the transition of one factory job from Paterson, New Jersey to Matamoros, Mexico, a city just across the Rio Grande that forms part of the US/Mexico border. Corporations make decisions about the future of employment and production locations based on financial analyses aimed at enriching shareholders. Management no longer has a compelling reason to keep local people employed. Mollie earned $7.61 per hour, her Mexican replacement Balbina 65 cents. Factory relocations are encouraged by neoliberal trade policies such as the North American Free Trade Agreement (NAFTA) which opens up cities like Matamoros to the *maquiladora* (assembly plant) economy. As the USA and other nations of the global North export their jobs to the global South, workers become easily replaced or simply surplus to requirements. Unemployment and wage stagnation are the result (Perrucci and Perrucci, 2008). US wages have not risen in real terms since the 1970s, even as American workers became more productive. But ordinary workers do not receive any extra benefit from working harder or more effectively. Company management and stockholders receive it instead. Business process outsourcing or 'offshoring' extends this dynamic from manufacturing to services work, as telecommunications technologies allow the fairly seamless movement of back office and telephonic work to cheaper wage regions such as India and Sri Lanka (Blinder, 2006). If you're laid off in the North it is often hard to find work that is as well paid as your prior job. A post-industrial services economy creates a lot of dead-end, poorly paid, insecure jobs with no career headroom: retail, cleaning and security; data entry; coffee-chain 'barista'.

In an effort to create jobs and boost economic activity, local and national governments have done all they can to attract inward investment from overseas. Japan experienced a prolonged economic boom in the 1980s and many of its corporations opened new production facilities in Western Europe, USA and Canada (Milkman, 1991). Investment was lured in by local governments offering 'sweeteners' to attract corporations to these locations, such as tax breaks, the construction of access roads and other forms of corporate welfare. The exact same dynamic takes place in the North as described in Klein's (2010: 194–229) damning writings about free economic zones in countries such as Honduras or the Philippines. A mighty transnational capitalist class simply leverages its huge power to make governments roll over and accept their demands. Why wouldn't they? Multinational corporations also make great play of threatening to leave host nations. Major banks were the focus of public outrage in the fallout from the 2007–8 financial crash. But if specific pressures were placed on them in terms of re-regulation and banking reform, their top management responded by saying they'll decamp to other cities with less stringent constraints.

This banking crisis created huge government budget deficits. Market globalizers demanded 'austerity measures' to address the deficits: cutbacks in welfare, education, health services and local government. And yet – ridiculously – government aid to private business (what critics describe as 'corporate welfare') is still handed out in billions of dollars per year. According to Left-leaning academics and politicians, global corporations such as Wal-Mart, Nissan, or Pfizer receive tax breaks and other supplements worth perhaps as much as 100 billion US dollars per year. Analysis published in *The Guardian* newspaper suggested that annual tax breaks and subsidies in the UK amount to £93 billion (Chakrabortty, 2015). (The claims were predictably rubbished by market globalizers.) Protest group US Uncut has exposed a range of corporate welfare programmes: tax breaks for corporate jets and CEO bonuses, subsidies to oil and pharmaceutical giants, bailouts for failed banks and insurers (Cahill, 2015).

Taxpayer handouts to corporations, along with the relaxation of regulations over trade, currency exchange and labour protection are all closely connected to neoliberal ideologies about shareholder primacy. According to this relatively new logic, corporations exist simply for the purposes of enriching shareholders. If more value for shareholders can be created by closing down production facilities in the North and opening them in the South then these changes are going to happen. Why would corporate management care about local jobs or communities if the governments regulating these places won't make the environment as permissive as possible for the generation of shareholder wealth? Management and labour have always experienced conflict, of course. But globalization, according to its critics, has intensified their differences in interest, opening up a gulf between workers and the owners of capital. This serves to increase ordinary people's sense of powerlessness, particularly as governments will do all they can to accommodate corporations' demands (Badiou, 2016: 13–22).

Management's disconnection from workers is at its most extreme in the so-called 'Anglo-Saxon' variety of capitalism in the USA and UK where the doctrine of shareholder primacy is at its most intense. The ideology of market globalism fails to acknowledge any problems with this scenario, claiming that globalization simply makes economic restructuring and ceaseless change inevitable. But critics have argued that the shareholder-owned publicly listed company is just one possible form that a corporation can take (see, for example, Noam Chomsky's writings about worker-owned cooperatives, 2012: 34–6). Moreover, there is considerable variation in custom and practice around the world; German corporations are run (theoretically at least) on the basis of 'codetermination' whereby the interests of the executive board of directors are to some extent balanced by a supervisory board made up of other stakeholders, especially employees and unions. Japanese companies historically have not placed shareholder value at the summit of their hierarchy of interests, and are therefore very reluctant to engage in restructuring that might impact negatively on their core workforces (McCann, 2014a).

But even here, market globalism is 'without question the dominant ideology of our time' which has been 'disseminated worldwide by global power elites' (Steger, 2013: 106). The rhetorical force of the argument that there is no alternative to free markets and shareholder value is extremely powerful. Globalization 'clarifies and cuts through', just like the profit motive as explained by the fictional corporate takeover artist Gordon Gekko in the 1987 Oliver Stone movie *Wall Street*:

> The point is, ladies and gentlemen, that greed – for lack of a better word – is good. Greed is right. Greed works. Greed clarifies, cuts through, and captures the essence of the evolutionary spirit. Greed, in all of its forms – greed for life, for money, for love, knowledge – has marked the upward surge of mankind. (Gordon Gekko's speech to Teldar Paper stockholders, *Wall Street*, dir. Oliver Stone, 1987)

Supporters of global capitalism would never put it in quite these words, but the idea that competition and the profit motive drive progress and growth in society is the basic message of the globalization mainstream, hammered home repeatedly by *The Wall Street Journal, The Economist, Forbes* magazine, or *Business Week*. Globalization basically works for everyone and the wealth trickles down. We've seen how socialism and communism fail. There is no better system available. Yes, some people will have to endure job loss at certain points, but to argue that globalization destroys jobs is to miss the bigger picture. Jobs in agriculture have disappeared in their tens of millions due to economic and technological change over the twentieth century, but this doesn't mean that all former farmworkers in the North are chronically unemployed, on welfare or dead. Displaced people find jobs in other sectors that have grown. The same will be true for downsized industrial workers (Wolf, 2004: 179–80).

But, no matter how many times this message is repeated – no matter how many times we're instructed that globalization is good for everybody, that wealth is trickling down and that all developments represent rational, inevitable progress – many will never believe it. And they will probably be right. This is because every day people are confronted by yet further evidence of rising economic inequality and declining democratic scrutiny of global elites. Critics argue that the top echelons of society seem to be getting ever more wealthy and ever more arrogant, corrupt and divorced from everyday reality (Klein, 2017). The twin trends of increasing inequality and decreasing elite accountability seem to be worsening and will be explored in turn in the following sections.

The 'rediscovery' of inequality

Inequality (in income, life chances, health, education, housing, status and influence) has been a contentious problem for much of human history. The World Bank's mission statement is 'Working for a World Free of Poverty', with similar aims stated by charities and civil society groups such as the 2005 'Make Poverty History' campaign. But the Biblical phrase 'the poor are always with us' is well-founded. With the increasing technological sophistication and integration of a globalized world, the issue of wealth inequality seems increasingly severe.

We are not just discussing inequality between rich and poor nations, but inequality within them. Income inequality has recently been rediscovered as a major issue in policy circles, media and academia. High-profile social democratic or liberal politicians across many countries often talk of the need to address a crisis in income inequality and a collapse of social mobility. Critical academic texts such as Piketty's *Capital in the Twenty-First Century* (2014), Milanovic's *Global Inequality* (2016), and Stiglitz's *The Price of Inequality* (2013) have been widely read and debated. Few in the US seem to believe anymore in an idealistic 'American Dream' of upwards mobility for everyone who works hard (Perrucci and Perrucci, 2008).

Extremes of wealth inequality are not new. In earlier phases of industrial growth in the nineteenth century, the so-called 'robber barons' such as Carnegie or Rockefeller earned spectacular fortunes when there was no real oversight or regulation of capitalism. The Wall Street Crash of 1929 led to significant government regulation and the post-Second World War era saw broad-based economic growth with falls in inequality in many countries. But neoliberal globalization from the 1980s onwards has seen inequality once again on the rise, with some comparing today's corporate elites to the nineteenth century 'robber barons'. A simple political slogan capturing this sense of inequality and remoteness is the notion of 'the 1%' (the global elites with their ever-increasing wealth and power) versus 'the 99%' (everyone else with next-to-nothing).

For the general population, the 99 percent [...] it's been pretty harsh [...] For the 1 percent and even less – the one-tenth of 1 percent – it's just fine. They are richer than ever, more powerful than ever, controlling the political system, disregarding the public. (Chomsky, 2012: 32)

This situation is tacitly admitted in some of the artefacts of the 1%, such as a 2005 investment report by a trio of Citigroup financial analysts which described a 'Plutonomy' of the super-rich with almost all the planet's assets while everyone else was more or less excluded and poor (Chomsky, 2012: 32). Those looking for investment opportunities are advised to focus on the Plutonomy – the rest are irrelevant. This infamous report is entitled 'Plutonomy: Buying luxury, explaining global imbalances' (Kapur et al., 2005) and can be found pretty easily on the internet. It's no secret that globalization 'grants indecent levels of impunity to the ultrarich' (Klein, 2017: 258). It's all pretty much there in plain sight.

The obviousness of global inequality and the remoteness and indifference of elites is probably due in part to the neoliberal agenda in global economic policy (Ray, 2007). Critics claim that the single-minded championing of economic growth as if it is the only possible concern for governments and citizens has narrowed the perspective of pro-globalization policy-makers and experts to such a degree that the application of market ideology comes before any consideration of context, democracy or basic common sense (Mishra, 2016; Stiglitz, 2002). Government intervention is 'proven' to be bad for growth, so welfare provision is cut back. In the South, 'structural adjustment' or 'conditionalities' applied to aid or loans from the global North have enforced the reduction of government spending in less-developed nations (Glennie, 2008). Loans can create chronic debt and deprive national governments of the capacity to manage their own affairs. Structural adjustment allows powerful multinationals to buy up and manage a developing country's oil, gas or water assets, often repatriating profits overseas. Developing countries are no longer allowed to put up tariffs or use other means to protect their industries from global competition (Chang, 2003). But World Bank and IMF economic analysis insists that neoliberal policies will liberate economies from excessive bureaucracy and will allow free trade to flourish, creating jobs and growth.

The issue here is that economic growth does not always mean poverty reduction. Many countries have experienced economic growth without poverty reduction, and almost all have seen economic growth coupled with increasing inequality. 'Jobless growth' has become a problem in the South just as it has in the North. Jonathan Glennie gives the example of an aluminium smelter in Mozambique which helps to boost Mozambique's GDP figures but doesn't contribute much to reducing the poverty of ordinary locals (Glennie, 2008: 79). 'A rise in a nation's overall wealth says nothing about equality *within* that nation' (Perry, 2008: 25). In the 1990s, world income grew by 2.5 per cent annually, but the total number of people living in poverty increased by almost 100 million (Stiglitz, 2002: 9). It is estimated that the three richest individual people in the world own more wealth than the combined GDP of the 48 poorest countries (Perry, 2008: 323). Recent research has suggested average pre-tax income of the bottom 50% of the US population has stagnated at around $16,000 per year from 1980–2014, a fall in the share of national income from 20% to 12%. Over the same period the average pre-tax income of the top 1% rose from $420,000 to $1.3 million, representing a growth of the share of total income from 12% to 20% (Piketty et al., 2016: 3).

Anti-globalization protests or the 'alter-globalization' movement has often reflected the powerlessness of ordinary people in the face of global elites. Street protests against the annual meetings of the WTO, World Economic Forum and IMF as well as the rise of the critical alternative World Social Forum in the late 1990s and early 2000s created a lot of discussion and media interest. But the protests and statements of the globalization critics were typically portrayed by mainstream media as incoherent, wrong-headed and basically irrelevant. Certain actions have created spectacular images and headlines, such as the 'bossnappings' and physical attacks by workers on business executives in France, including an infamous incident in 2015 where Air France managers had their suits and shirts torn by protestors and had to be rushed to safety by security guards. Redundancies and workforce lockouts in China have often seen large-scale confrontations between laid-off workers and their management. It's great drama, but what's the point? All it seems to do is draw attention to the powerlessness or perhaps irrelevance of ordinary people.

Workers have become surplus to the requirements of global capitalism. In China, mass downsizings of former state-owned factories took place because these plants may have played important roles in the old Communist planned economy, but have no place in globally integrated product markets. Neoliberal reforms in Russia after the Soviet collapse led to large-scale and prolonged downsizing in Russia. Entire industrial sectors that had stagnated during the Soviet decline in the 1980s then collapsed in little more than the first few years of the 1990s. Ordinary people can show their disgust with economic policies that threaten their livelihoods but ultimately they have little recourse other than to somehow adapt and survive. That's the crux of the matter. Arguments and policies are made in economic terms ('the plant in Rotherham or Lordstown is closing because the price of steel production is too high in Britain or the US'), but people construct their worldview more in moral arguments ('how can you sleep at night having made thousands of your loyal workers redundant?'). Moral arguments just aren't forthcoming from the global market elites. 'You are no longer of use to the global economy – stop moaning and learn to deal with it'.

The 99% makes concession after concession. But the global corporations want more. Free trade deals release further controls over them. Corporations and transnational financial organizations have effectively run countries and overridden governments in the developing world for many years (Glennie, 2008). Now they're starting to do this in the developed world, too. Privatization, austerity and cutbacks have meant the handing over of core government functions to private contractors (Badiou, 2016: 16–22; Klein, 2007; 2010: xix–xxii). The proposed trade and investment deal known as the Comprehensive Economic and Trade Agreement (CETA) between Canada and the EU provides for the establishment of corporate courts, basically lifting the legal system up and out of national control and into some sort of global twilight zone beyond the influence of citizen voters. To the market globalists this is simply harmonization and efficiency providing a level playing field for trade and growth. To global critics it's an affront to democracy. Under certain definitions, international business corporations are now starting to carve out for themselves the same rights as people – something called 'corporate personhood'. Corporations lobby to establish laws that make it illegal for governments to restrict corporate actions even while governments have been cutting back on state spending to try to tackle budget deficits in the wake of a financial crisis caused by the likes of Citibank, Lehman Brothers and AIB. In 2010 the tobacco corporation Philip Morris sued the government of Uruguay for enacting tougher anti-smoking legislation. The corporation claimed the new anti-smoking laws devalue its brand names and investments in that country. It lost the case. But civil society groups such as Global Justice Now or War on Want argue that the establishment of corporate courts or 'Investor-State Dispute Resolutions' such as the one proposed in CETA would embolden MNCs to try further actions like this.

This, according to the critics of globalization, is where the doctrine of neoliberalism leaves us. We are told there is no alternative to free markets and free trade and that these policies work for everyone. But in reality they've achieved little for the poor and a lot for the (already) rich while eroding all forms of democratic accountability. The political elite has been compromised by its deep involvement in facilitating this global corporate takeover and is thus totally unresponsive to ordinary peoples' concerns (Klein, 2017). '[T]he system of democracy has been shredded' suggests Chomsky (2012: 54) and it's hard to disagree. The challenges of poverty and precarious work, coupled with the sense of being let down both by globalization and by local political processes that are supposed to represent ordinary people, creates an alienated and disenfranchised constituency which might be tempted by a rabble-rouser such as Donald Trump and his particular brand of right-wing anti-globalization rhetoric. Struggling to make ends meet? Feel left behind? Then blame the immigrants for taking your jobs, the government bureaucrats for wasting your taxes, the media for not telling you the truth and the politicians for ignoring your concerns. Thus, the billion-aire Trump presents himself as a man of the people seeking common ground with workers in attacking globalization and free trade. 'Globalization has made the financial elite who donate to politicians very, very wealthy' shouts Trump, 'but it has left millions of our workers with nothing but poverty and heartache' (Jackson, 2016). This is almost exactly what Noam Chomsky says at Occupy rallies.

With critique of global corporations and their highly supportive and enabling politician friends becoming mainstream in the traditional political Right as well as the Left, one wonders why nothing really changes. There are always more poor people in the world than rich. So how does the elite cling to power? Why aren't the politicians who support neoliberal globalization voted out of office and replaced by socialists or economic nationalists of some kind who will defend local jobs and wrest back control from the market globalist elites? Critics will argue that globalization provides powerful means for the global power elite to limit the influence of local or national power over them, a very troublesome issue that we will now turn to.

Where is the accountability? Is anyone in control of globalization?

Alongside the indignation at the supposed greed and remoteness of global elites, more moderate critics claim that global wealth inequality has reached such levels that even the wealthy will come to regret the extremes (Stiglitz, 2013). Part of the explanation for the disastrous global banking collapse of 2007–8 was the lack of savings and credit-worthiness of so many new homeowners who had been mis-sold mortgages they could not really afford. Inequality is dysfunctional to the whole economy. This element of critique of economic globalization – its riskiness, its casino-like nature – is often made by both the anti-globalist critics and by the more mainstream globalist writers (such as, for example, Giddens, 1991; 1999). This is because the chaos and volatility of economic globalization poses threats to *everyone*, including the 'Plutonomy', the 1% or the global transnational class. Hyperglobalization since the roaring nineties has been stalked by the spectres of risk and disorder, and dangers are multiplied by international interconnections such as global financial risks, crises and shocks that have become 'systemic' (Centino and Cohen, 2010; Holton, 2012; Stiglitz, 2002). The global financial architecture is now so wide, so deep, so accelerated and so poorly regulated (witness 'shadow banking', 'high-frequency trading', 'flash crashes', 'off-balance sheet' activities) that it is increasingly difficult for anyone to control it (Virilio, 2012b: 12–13).

This pervasive viewpoint, that no-one is really in control of globalization, fits the earlier literature on 'risk society' to a large extent (Beck, 1992; Giddens, 1990), as well as Bauman's notion of the liquidity of global networks and flows (Bauman, 2000; see also Ritzer, 2010). But this view can be dangerous in that it obscures from view some of the real powers that *are* used to control the global economy to a very considerable extent and the degree to which many major organizations have no incentive to, for example, create a workable and enforceable global ban on landmines, close tax loopholes or to finally agree on effective curbs on greenhouse emissions. Some would claim there is a central core, a centre of gravity, or a 'power elite' that carefully chooses which resources to expend in efforts to realize its own selfish aims; an elite that controls, obstructs and confuses, all the while denying it has any of the influence that its critics ascribe to it (Mills, 1956/2000). This is not to descend into some paranoid and idiotic conspiracy theory of a secretive world-running Bilderberg group, or an anti-Semitic diatribe against 'ZOG' (a supposed 'Zionist Occupational Government'). But it would be to make an important point that such an abstract, sanitized and depoliticized view of risks, flows and liquids can be vague and can divert our attention from the real power-brokers and elites of society, characters who don't want their conduct publicly exposed (Pilger, 2016). There is a global elite or transnational capitalist class (Sklair, 2000) that does a very good job of promoting its own interests, often at the expense of other, weaker groups. Government agencies such as military, police and foreign services can also be involved in shadowy operations such as state-sponsored terrorism, misinformation campaigns, electronic snooping and various other abuses of power (Ellsberg, 2004). The so-called global 'war on terror' – US President George W. Bush's reaction to the 9/11 terrorist attacks – was deeply implicated in questionable practices that amounted to political repression. This included holding terror suspects without trial or charge and the practice of 'extraordinary rendition' whereby detainees were secretly shipped to other 'black sites' for 'enhanced interrogation', i.e. torture (Chwastiak, 2015; Hill, 2008). Although many would argue that globalization threatens and erodes the nation state, new technologies provide new vistas of opportunity for states and corporations involved in the global business of war: this includes global digital technologies of electronic surveillance and unmanned drones that can gather intelligence and attack targets remotely. Investigative journalist William Arkin (2015: 23–6) describes a sinister and globally extensive new 'Data Machine' operated by the US military and its corporate partners, a huge intersection of software and technology platforms with conspiratorial-sounding codenames such as Gilgamesh, Thunderbunny, Goldminer, ECHELON and Prism.

Interestingly, however, in a 'global' society it may be becoming harder to hide such abuses. The general public can now find out a great deal about extraordinary rendition, torture and electronic surveillance by using some of the same global technologies established by the military–industrial complex. A famous irony of globalization is that the origin of some of the concepts and systems of the internet itself lies with ARPANET, a computer network developed for use by the US Defense Department's Advanced Research Projects Agency. In the early 1970s, the top-secret Pentagon Papers about America's war in Vietnam were laboriously photocopied by hand and secretly passed to newspaper reporters and Congressmen (Ellsberg, 2004). In the 2000s, hacked and leaked Iraq War-related military logs and US diplomatic cables were simply uploaded in their thousands to websites such as Wikileaks where they remain for public scrutiny. Individuals involved in the illicit gathering and publicizing of classified government documents may be prosecuted by state authorities, but once the files are 'out there' on the internet there is no going back. Wikileaks has even developed a searchable online database containing profiles of people who may work for clandestine services so that concerned citizens can 'watch the watchers'. Such is the risk of security breaches in a hyper-digitized world that Russian intelligence services have supposedly gone back to using typewriters and manual records for some areas of their work (Irvine, 2013).

There are good reasons to question the conduct of elites which claim to govern globalization in an increasingly ungovernable world. Five years after the terrorist attacks of 2001, *FT* journalist and former World Bank economist Martin Wolf proclaimed that the forces behind globalization have 'won the day' and have performed 'heroically' (Wolf, 2006). Although he did concede the possibility that some new crisis might derail global capital he didn't give the reader the impression that he believed that it would. He was by no means the only analyst to have been caught out by the dramatic events of 2007–8 in which the collapse of the US housing market brought down much of the world's highly interconnected and over-leveraged financial system. Global losses were estimated in terms of *trillions* of dollars and the global banking, insurance and credit-rating agencies went through years of turmoil, recriminations and soul-searching. Trying to calculate the 'true' financial size of such a drastic collapse with so many interconnecting features and varying definitions is almost as difficult a task as trying to define globalization itself. Estimates have ranged from 6 to 14 trillion USD, with some economists suggesting it might take until 2023 until world economic activity returns to its pre-2007 levels. Schools, hospitals, social care, policing and other vital public services saw their funding cut back as government spending was severely curtailed by 'austerity measures' put in to try to curb budgetary deficits. So much for the 'heroism' of free markets.

The global economic crash of 2007–8 and the subsequent cutbacks and austerity measures have generated a widespread feeling that powerful corporate and government interests do exist and are, to some extent, identifiable. It's not that *no-one* is in control. It's more that the elites are increasingly remote from ordinary people and therefore can't be held to account. Global corporate and political organizations are often very unpopular, as shown in countless public opinion surveys that suggest powerful elite groups are not widely trusted. Financial crises, political scandals, weakening incomes and costly and bloody wars throughout the 1990s and 2000s have been at the heart of a wellspring of protest movements that have emerged across many societies, from the anti-globalization movement that came to prominence at the WTO conference in Seattle in 1999, to the various protests that developed in the wake of the 2007–8 global financial crash, such as the 15M movement and the 'Indignados' protesting against austerity measures in Spain; the 99% and Occupy movements that began in Zuccotti Park, New York City; and the so-called 'Arab Spring'. Typically beginning life as local movements in response to local grievances, in recent years some of these protests have taken on 'global' features in their widespread use of social media organizing tactics, perhaps most notably the 'Arab Spring' campaigns of 2010–16 that triggered substantial political upheavals in Tunisia, Egypt and Bahrain. While the contexts, members and outcomes of these movements can differ considerably, the grievances tend to be similar: ordinary people feel disempowered in the face of remote and unresponsive governments that are more interested in representing global elites such as banks, industrial corporations and militaries rather than ordinary citizens, resulting in increasingly outrageous inequalities in wealth and an absence of democratic representation. A Tumblr blog entitled 'We are the 99%' (wearethe99percent.tumblr.com) became a kind of electronic base-station for the disaffected, especially the young who own no financial assets and face the dim prospects of chronic unemployment; low pay; rising housing, health and education costs and no realistic political candidates who speak to their interests and concerns. Political systems, parties and elected representatives are 'captured' by the financial power and incessant lobbying of international elites and are thus thoroughly corrupted and debased (Chomsky, 2012).

The obvious response is for disenfranchised ordinary people to club together, organize, protest and get their message out. Tireless critics of neoliberal globalization such as Klein, Chomsky and Pilger claim that resistance is far from futile: 'from very simple things up to starting a new socio-economic system with worker and community-run enterprises, a whole range of things are possible' (Chomsky, 2012: 72). But what power and resources do they have? Multivariate analysis by US political scientists Gilens and Page (2014) suggested that large corporations and their well-organized, well-resourced and deeply entrenched lobby groups have substantial influence over policy-making in Washington. Local, grassroots, community-funded groups, on the other hand, have practically zero influence. Certainly the things that Chomsky calls for are *possible*. But would they make any difference? The next section explores this issue, suggesting the prospects are not encouraging.

Cycles of critique – how critiques of globalization become part of globalization

Reading through this chapter you might think that everyone in the world hates globalization. You'd almost be right. Criticism of global inequalities, risks and rampant consumerism are hardly extreme positions. To a large degree, they are actually taken for granted and obvious. One might even say criticism is part of the mainstream (Appelbaum and Robinson, 2005; Latour, 2004). Anti-globalization sentiments play well commercially. Mid-1990s' literature and film such as *Fight Club, American Psycho* and *The Beach* were critically and commercially successful. *The Beach* was a British novel made into a Hollywood blockbuster starring Leonardo DiCaprio as a disaffected youth looking for an 'authentic' or 'alternative' travel experience away from commercialism. He stumbles upon a group of countercultural misfits which has found the perfect beach community separate from corporate-run 'adventure' holidays where Generation X-ers can 'find themselves'. Ironically, DiCaprio and the Twentieth Century Fox production crew were heavily criticized by local civil society groups in Thailand for damaging the local ecosystem while shooting on location. To make the film, this 'unspoilt' beach was affected by erosion, defoliation and the planting of non-native coconut trees. Local environmentalists brought a lawsuit against the Thai forestry department for allowing this ecological destruction to take place (*BBC News*, 2000).

More notoriously, corporate and consumerist excess was viciously criticized in Bret Easton Ellis' *American Psycho* (1991), a satire on the brand names, consumerism and moral emptiness of global capitalism. The anti-hero protagonist is Patrick Bateman, a 27-year-old Wall Street investment banker who lives in the exclusive American Gardens building on West 81st Street. A murderous psychopath, he pointlessly slaughters colleagues, prostitutes, children and vagrants, sometimes keeping grisly trophies of his victims in top-of-the-line refrigerators across a series of desirable apartments. Bateman's monologues about mineral water, beauty products and Phil Collins brilliantly expose the meaninglessness of the cultural products of the global economy. Towards the end of the book his character kind of disappears or 'melts into air', his gross crimes going somehow unnoticed, symbolizing the total lack of accountability and remoteness of financial elites from the society they are slowly killing. Bateman muses to the reader:

> [...] there is an idea of a Patrick Bateman, some kind of abstraction, but there is no real me, only an entity, something illusory, and though I can hide my cold gaze and you can shake my hand and feel flesh gripping yours and maybe you can even sense our lifestyles are probably comparable: *I simply am not there.* (Ellis, 1991: 362)

The point here is that the message of these books and films – the critique of global consumerism – has itself become 'cool' and marketable. Global business is acutely aware of the critique; people are tired of McDonaldized mass production offerings. Sophisticated consumers (young people in particular) want something that speaks to them, an 'authentic' product or experience that acknowledges concerns around ecology and maybe helps build capacity for Sumatran coffee-growing cooperatives. Counter-culture is co-opted into the mainstream. All hail the hipster, vintage clothing and high-end bicycle workshops. Brands have become 'ethical' (Egan-Wyer et al., 2014). Global multinationals are lowering their carbon footprint, acting sustainably, listening to their consumers as well as their workers and supervisors – sorry, I mean their 'people' and 'team leaders'. Leadership and branding consultants increasingly sell a story of dumping brands and 'getting real'. Naomi Klein herself has to resist the temptation to copyright and leverage her 'No Logo' logo (Klein, 2010: xvi). In 2003 the 'culture-jamming' anti-corporate *Adbusters* magazine started selling the 'Blackspot Sneaker', its own 'signature brand of "subversive" running shoes' (Heath and Potter, 2006: 3). Cynical tech-savvy professionals working in the financial industry produce websites criticizing the greed and recklessness of their own industry (see, for example, www.zerohedge.com). Notions of 'post-capitalism' and 'universal basic income' moved from the counterculture into neoliberal policy (see Chapter 5).

Global capitalism is now so self-aware and so effortlessly dominant that it can criticize its own products and ideology while continuing to make money. The business and leadership guru Tom Peters in a *Fast Company* article seemed to freely admit that much of his bestselling leadership book *In Search of Excellence* was made up; even his 'confessions' about this 20 years later seemed designed to maximize media attention rather than provide practical business advice (Peters, 2001). What use is such commercialized 'knowledge' in a so-called knowledge economy? Does it differ from pop culture? Would that even matter? There is an idea of a Tom Peters, some kind of abstraction.

As we arrive at the end of this chapter on the critics of globalization, what I hope to have shown is that criticisms of and resistances to globalization are very much part of the ideology and practice of neoliberal globalization (Mittelman, 2004). Globalization – because the notion is so all-encompassing and its logic so circular – becomes an almost inescapable idea, maybe an inescapable reality. This is perhaps another reason to reject the most strident forms of global scepticism explored in Chapter 2. The next chapter will move on to explore cultural globalization, where these notions of critique and cyclicality take on a whole new dimension in the transfer, spread, adoption, rejection and hybridization of so-called 'global culture'.

4

The Globalization Culture Wars

Globalization starts wars.

(Perry, 2008: 227)

If the 1990s marked the expansion of globalized opportunity then the 2000s will probably be remembered as a decade of struggle, conflict and tragedy. The twenty-first century opened with the juddering halt of the 1990s tech-stock boom as dotcom companies were exposed as hugely overvalued. Major accounting scandals and financial frauds came to light, bringing down corporations such as Enron and WorldCom – former poster children for the digital, internet-driven New Economy. And in September 2001 an event took place that was so shocking and dramatic that many found it almost incomprehensible.

> Tuesday, September 11, 2001, dawned temperate and nearly cloud-less in the eastern United States. Millions of men and women readied themselves for work. Some made their way to the Twin Towers, the signature structures of the World Trade Center in New York City. Others went to Arlington, Virginia, to the Pentagon. [...] For those heading to an airport, weather conditions could not have been better for a safe and pleasant journey. (9/11 Commission, 2004: 1)

The *Final Report of the National Commission on Terrorist Attacks Upon the United States* doesn't read like most government reports I'm familiar with. It's cinematic, mirroring the drama and tragedy of the 9/11 atrocities. 24/7 rolling news had been a fact of life since the 1990s – footage of exploding airliners and collapsing towers were repeated end-lessly around the world. New York City – as befitting its role as perhaps the quintessential 'global' metropolis – was criss-crossed by intersecting angles of video recording, meaning the World Trade Center towers' col-lapse was captured across an array of sources: CCTV security cameras, professional news media, tourists' camcorders, even by webcams that fed a postmodern art installation (Hill, 2008: 7). Eyewitnesses or the horrified millions watching live TV news made allusions to far-fetched

Hollywood action movies such as *Die Hard*, *The Towering Inferno* or *Armageddon* as they attempted to put what they saw into words. A few high-profile artists and musicians made unguarded comments about the imagery and orchestration of 9/11 being 'stunning' before quickly issuing apologies (Hill, 2008: 8–9).

9/11 and the subsequent 'war on terror' have come to feature heavily in the globalization literature. This is because the rise of 'global networks' of terrorist organizations aiming to attack and terrify ordinary civilians seem to be related somehow to a pushback or 'blowback' effect against the steady encroachment of Western-led globalization of economy, politics and especially culture (Barber, 1992; Johnson, 2002). Moreover, the extraordinary hypermediation of the attacks on New York and Washington, DC possess powerful cultural resonance in themselves. The appalling images of death and destruction are literally unforgettable; the atrocious scale and visibility of the attacks on the US's centres of economic and military power were stupefying. Terrorism has always leveraged image and shock value in its attempts to provoke a political reaction, but Al-Qaeda's 'planes operation' was extraordinarily dramatic: a multi-sited terror attack combined with the instantaneity and reach of global news media and the internet age to make the largest possible impact. The intensity of the imagery provided a rich mine for further exploitation and allusion. Staring out somehow more forcefully than the other 18 mugshots of the hijackers, there seemed something especially unnerving about the lead operative Mohammad Atta, whose image was seized on by media sources accustomed to presenting a 'face of pure evil' like Myra Hindley or Charles Manson. Images of terror, violence and conflict present a prominent, and deeply unpleasant, form of global culture.

The 'global war on terror' that has dragged on in various forms ever since the 9/11 attacks is to a large extent a media war, conducted not just via government sources and corporate news media channels but also increasingly by homemade and independently circulated social media (der Derian, 2009). The promotion and condemnation of terror, violence, its threat and its baleful consequences are continually re-enacted through video messages, Facebook pages and memorializing websites. Bizarre conspiracy theories about 9/11 are presented in home-made documentary films. Video games such as *Call of Duty* play out fantasies of hunting down terrorists in secretive and vengeful 'black' operations. Al Qaeda and more recently ISIS made sophisticated use of social media in glorifying terror attacks and recruiting further volunteers to the jihadist cause, often in ways that mimicked the violent noise and imagery of Hollywood action movies.

9/11 led to an international outpouring of cultural products such as fiction, music, film, journalism and academic theorizing. Much of the Western content reflected the sense of generalized anxiety, loss and bewilderment emanating from this disaster, sometimes verging towards the absurd in trying to explain this seemingly impossible event, from Don de Lillo's novel *Falling Man* to Jarett Kobek's *ATTA,* a fictionalized life-history of the most infamous of the 9/11 attackers. The 9/11 Commission report speculated at one point that the idea for a 'suicide hijack' might have come from a Tom Clancy novel (9/11 Commission, 2004: 347).

The 'global war on terror', the emergence of ISIS and the frequent recurrence of terrorist attacks across much of the world highlight the ways in which the increasing connectivity of globalization, while typically talked up by first wave global literature as progressive, humane and just, actually services to enable and intensify the nastiest and most divisive aspects of human life. Themes of creativity, efficiency, optimism, wealth-generation and interconnectivity that characterized the first wave globalization literature have been superseded by themes of global calamity, conflict, risk, xenophobia, racism, terrorism, violence and war. Globalization – far from uniting the world under the banners of democracy and capitalism – actually makes it easier to spread fear, to make war, to stimulate resentment and blowback, to provoke further division, hatred and violence. From the 2000s onwards terror, irrationality, violence and war have become central to how globalization is understood in academic and journalistic accounts. Globalization terror stories strangely mix the violent with the commercial in an endless generative spiral. Every day sees yet further terror-related tabloid fodder and internet clickbait: 'news' stories about 'jihadi brides' from Sweden; an ISIS recruitment video that rips off *Natural Born Killers;* the Atta mugshot somehow ending up in a bot-generated Facebook advert for car insurance in Texas.

Extremism and conflict are highly relevant to broader debates on global culture which form an important area of the globalization literature (Hopper, 2007; Nederveen Pieterse, 2009; Steger, 2013: 74–86). I use the phrase 'culture wars' in this chapter. Usually this term refers to long-running and acrimonious debates in the USA around social, cultural and political change since the 1960s relating to feminism, civil rights, ecology and the peace movement (Hartman, 2015). But the notion of culture wars also makes sense when connected to the literature and phenomena of globalization. This chapter will introduce the core debates of cultural globalization, showing how the increasing interconnectivity of the world is associated with both cultural integration and intercultural disharmony. The chapter begins by exploring the notion that globalization is creating an era of cultural homogenization and conformity. Some characterize global culture as a 'McWorld' of corporate, American-led consumerism; cultural differences and uniqueness are being driven out as human behaviour across the world is increasingly informed by a shared cultural script of Westernization, neoliberalism and democracy. It moves on to critique this position as superficial and largely inaccurate, introducing a diverse literature that instead describes global culture as a multitude of possibilities. The 'flows' of global culture come from many sources and have multiple impacts, including cultural hybridization, cultural mixing and the largely peaceful coexistence of diverse cultural formations. The literature then turns to issues of cultural conflict that many argue are stimulated or exacerbated by globalization, such as ethnic, religious and political violence, noting that globalization is (as ever) not mono-directional but rather always characterized by various forms of conflict, confusion, negotiation and contestation.

▬▬▬ 'McWorld' and its critics: Cultural globalization as corporate consumerism

Much of the globalization literature focuses primarily on its economic aspects but, even here, considerations of 'culture' feature in the commercial calculations of business and economy. Does an increasingly globalized world entail standardized product markets, or will global corporations enjoy success only if they tailor their products to local tastes? Much has been written, for example, about the struggles of MNCs' overseas operations in certain markets, such as the failure and closure of British grocery giant Tesco's 'Fresh and Easy' stores in the USA, or the weak performance of Starbucks in Australia where there had long been a culture of high-end coffee shops. On the other hand, many mass-market products are successfully sold across the world with little or no adaptation to local tastes, such as consumer electronics, running shoes, washing machines, toothpaste, video games and films.

The globalization literature has been heavily influenced by the symbolic power of the McDonald's fast food restaurant and the Nike swoosh. For many writers, globalization is best understood as a form of cultural imperialism; US-owned multinational corporations are reshaping the world in their image, driving out or suppressing local differences (Klein, 2010). Global corporate consumer capitalism is criticized in much of the literature. George Ritzer's famous McDonaldization writings portray a dumbed-down, standardized, sanitized and artificial world, in which the corporate logic of the fast food restaurant – efficiency, narrow choice and speed of delivery – increasingly intrudes into all areas of life around the globe and suppresses local uniqueness, spontaneity and genuine creativity (Ritzer, 2007; 2014). Alan Bryman similarly bemoans the deadening effects of the Walt Disney Corporation's cultural imperialism (1999). But others celebrate the spread of corporate cultural globalization, regarding it as logical, progressive and enthusiastically welcomed around the world. It can even act as a delivery system for liberty, stability, democracy and peace. Thomas Friedman (1999: 248–75) coined his 'Golden Arches Theory of Conflict Prevention' whereby no two countries where McDonald's has a market presence have ever gone to war with each another (although one can never be sure with Friedman if he means for his readers to take him entirely seriously). The McDonald's brand and all it entails has also clearly influenced another famous piece of global culture writing – Benjamin Barber's *Jihad vs. McWorld* article and subsequent book (1992, 2011). Barber is highly critical of a corporate-driven McWorld in a similar way to Ritzer and Bryman; the elements of his work regarding *jihad* will be reflected on later in this chapter. In Kobek's *ATTA* (2011: 78) the titular terrorist describes US consumerism as:

> The countless, fathomless Niagara of strip malls. They are all the same. Dunkin' Donuts, Taco Bell, Pizza Hut, McDonald's, Burger King, Wendy's, Radio Shack, Long John Silver's, Arby's, Hardee's, Krispy Kreme, Baskin-Robbins, Dippin' Dots, Carvel.

Bryman's work (1999) adds another element to Ritzer's critique of corporate homogenization by arguing that the principles and values of the Disney Corporation are increasingly being inscribed across global society. He identifies these as the intense theming of every product and service it provides, the reshaping of the mundane activity of shopping into a deeper, broader and ideologically infused 'customer experience'; aggressive merchandising and brand saturation; and the proactive management of highly scripted customer experiences by staff trained to manage customers' emotions. Bryman's critique of Disney lies not so much along the lines of Ritzer's attack on McDonalds' ruthless pursuit of efficiency, calculability, predictability and control. It is more to do with the tacky and slightly unnerving promotion of Disney's 'values' to the world; the sheer volume and power of Disney-type value-projection amounts to a global onslaught of American cultural indoctrination that is difficult to ignore or counteract.

These criticisms are not new, but globalization seems to intensify them. From the 1940s through to the 1960s, Frankfurt School theorists

Adorno, Horkheimer and Marcuse attacked the rise of a 'culture industry' that provides a narrow and propagandized cultural script for
people to follow and reproduce (see Adorno and Horkheimer,
1987/2002: 94–136). Classic writings of leftists such as Noam
Chomsky (2002) or the Glasgow University Media Group (1976) continued with themes of 'media control' or a 'propaganda model' in
which media content is systematically skewed to favour the interests of
corporate and political elites. These processes are strengthened by globalization and neoliberal deregulation, as governments sell off state-run
media providers and smaller cultural producers and publishers are
purchased by gigantic multimedia corporations such as Comcast, GE,
Newscorp, Disney, Viacom, Penguin Random House, Time Warner,
Sony and Google. Today the largest 'infotainment' corporations dominate US and international cultural output, with around 6–8 of the
largest corporations accounting for around two thirds of worldwide
communication industry revenues (Steger, 2013: 82). Their activities
range over TV and pay-per-view; film and animation studios; social
media platforms; online video-sharing channels; newspapers, maga-
zines, comics and books; educational content; radio stations; cellular
phones and broadband internet provision; and the distribution systems
for downloadable apps.

These developments raise fears over the increasing power of concen-
trated media ownership to set news agendas and thus unduly influence
the worldviews and actions of citizens and governments. Opinion polls
suggest that public trust in corporate news media is at historic lows.
Critics of globalized media corporations argue that consumers the
world over are being fed a diet of standardized trash produced by a
clique of producers creating highly commercialized US-led news and
cultural content (Lash and Lury, 2007). Output is typically dumbed
down and predominantly reflects socially conservative, pro-business
and pro-American positions. Such is the fear of being culturally overrun
that many national governments subsidize their own national film
industries to keep them alive or restrict overseas programming on their
TV stations (Martell, 2010 : 84).

Hemmed in by the McDonald's arches, seduced by the Disney smile
and caught in the beams of the Fox News searchlights, there is a strong
argument to be made that cultural globalization is primarily about corporate-driven homogenization and standardization; powerful MNCs
based in the richest countries of the world monopolize the production,
distribution and sale of media, consumer and cultural offerings in the
same way as they would try to do with any product market. The huge
scale and influence of McDonald's, Disney, Google, Bertelsmann,
Facebook, Fox News and Sony are almost impossible to counterbalance.

Critics argue that ordinary people have little real choice in what products to consume and what facts they believe to be true. To a large extent, of course, people freely choose to purchase McDonald's food, watch CNN or share their personal lives on Twitter. But given the power of corporate homogenization of global culture, this doctrine of 'customer choice' is illusory. People around the world can 'choose' only from a narrow menu because '[c]ulture today is infecting everything with sameness' (Adorno and Horkheimer, 1987/2002: 94). Rem Koolhaas (2002) famously derided contemporary cultural, organizational and architectural forms as 'Junkspace'. The global economy endlessly regurgitates non-spaces and non-activities, its cultural realm debased. Globalization is aesthetically and intellectually degenerate. 'Brands in Junkspace perform the same role as black holes in the universe: they are essences through which meaning disappears' (Koolhaas, 2002: 177). Many resent the intrusion of Western products, ideologies, brands and modes of existence. Disaffected citizen-consumers receive the bountiful goods of the global culture industry with reluctance, indifference, resistance or resigned compliance.

But it is here where the argument about the imposition of Western-led corporate global culture might reach its limits. If we accept that some people are disaffected and cynical about Disney or Fox News, then the supposedly homogenizing effects of global corporate culture might be exaggerated. How much does the widespread availability of global consumer products really affect cultures and behaviours around the world which are likely to be deeply ingrained (Hopper, 2007: 108)? Some major academic studies suggest that the impacts of cultural globalization are actually quite limited, and that national and subnational cultures remain robust and distinct. Political scientist Ronald Inglehart has worked for many years on his 'World Values Survey' that has aimed to track international and intergenerational changes in social values and behaviours. His most recent book (Norris and Inglehart, 2009) suggests that national cultures remain largely insulated from the potential changes one might expect from intensified Western-led corporate globalization. Cultural diversity is perhaps not as threatened by globalization as the 'culture industry' critics assume. Another famous contribution to academic research into large-scale cultural trends was Gert Hofstede's *Culture's Consequences* (2003) where Hofstede constructs six 'dimensions' of national culture across which cultural norms and behaviours can be measured and compared across countries, such as 'power distance', 'individuality versus collectivity' or 'indulgence versus restraint'. Hofstede tends to see rather limited changes to these dimensions over time, suggesting strong degrees of continuity of national culture despite the huge potential influence of globalization.

Debates around cultural imperialism extend well beyond the subject of the consumer products of the global economy. 'Global culture' debates penetrate deeply into notions of politics, identity, religion, behaviours and beliefs; it says something about the norms, values and traditions that people live by and how these might be changing in a global age. Manfred Steger notes the rise of the English language around the globe and the rapid decline of lesser-used languages that are sadly becoming extinct. Spoken languages in use worldwide have dropped from around 14,500 in 1500 to fewer than 6,500 today (Steger, 2013: 86). Linguistic diversity certainly seems to be a victim of the globalization of culture. This is certainly evidence of a contraction of cultural diversity as the global North dominates the processes of world integration. But does globalization really entail the collapse of all cultural difference into Western-dominated homogeneity? This would be taking the argument too far.

It is vital to note that the economic, political, and cultural influence of the global North and the USA are strongly challenged and possibly in decline. The media oligopoly of Fox News and MSNBC are countered by the rise of social media and by the rise of new global media players such as Russia Today, CCTV and Al Jazeera – the 24/7 news platforms of the rising powers of Russia, China and the Arabic world. While highly commercial and transnational, and with a production style that emulates those of 'world class' broadcasters like CNN, they often provide alternative news agendas and will sometimes explicitly market themselves as providing much-needed counterbalances to the US-driven mainstream. This tactic is particularly visible with RT. For example, recent global news stories exposing state-sponsored doping of Russian Olympic athletes were countered by similar allegations on RT about the use of performance-enhancing drugs by European and American competitors.

There are good reasons to be sceptical about the idea of a cultural imperialism or corporate neo-colonialism being projected from 'the West' upon 'the rest'. Grahame Thompson, for example, breezily dismisses the cultural impacts of the worldwide distribution of movies such as *RoboCop 3* (2014: 3). Cultural, religious, ethnic and national forms of identity can be remarkably durable. 'Global culture' is not just exported from the global North, but emerges from many sources and evolves in complex ways as it interacts with other cultural domains (Bhagwati, 2007: 106–21).

It is useful to consider the durability of local and national cultural forms and to be sceptical about the power of global culture to influence, unhinge or suppress them. The work of Hofstede and Inglehart, for example, provides plenty of evidence of the continued diversity of culture. However, this style of research often objectivizes and essentializes 'national culture', portraying 'culture' as a static, immutable trait of people and places – a limited way of thinking inherited from nineteenth and early twentieth century colonial thinking that tended to objectify and exoticize. It is perhaps more accurate and less condescending to regard 'culture' not as some form of fixed national character trait but as a highly dynamic, changing, contested and multivocal *process* (Hopper, 2007: 181; Jenkins, 2012). Notions of movement, fluidity, change and uncertainty as central features of human culture are prominent in the accounts of global culture authors who take a different position from the Ritzer or Bryman 'homogenization' argument. For writers such as Hannerz (1990), Nederveen Pieterse (1995, 2009) and Kelts (2006), globalization is not about cultural standardization or the diminution of diversity. Instead, globalization meets culture in a riot of creativity in which new hybrid cultures emerge. The next section explores these ideas.

Cowboys in Turkey: Remixing global culture

A major problem with McDonaldization, McWorld and media control arguments is that they tend to assume a one-directional process of continual colonization of passive global audiences. In so doing they almost certainly overstate the power of MNCs. They downplay the importance of the *reception* of imported cultural products (Martell, 2010: 94). Audiences are capable of ignoring, criticizing and distancing themselves from a US-led global pop culture that is supposedly infiltrating their lives. An interesting and original piece of audience-reception research was conducted by Ien Ang for her book *Watching Dallas* (1985), in which she gathered the opinions of Dutch TV audiences. *Dallas* was an iconic American TV series from the 1980s that was notorious for its celebratory portrayal of the opulent lifestyles of Texas oil company executives and their families. Views ranged from those who were openly critical of its trashiness, to others who regarded it as comic and ludicrous. There were even some rather philosophical viewers who seemed to regard the programme as at least partly self-critical:

> My opinion of *Dallas*? WORTHLESS RUBBISH. I find it a typical American programme, simple and commercial. (1985: 91)

> I find it amusing precisely because it's so ghastly. (1985: 99)

> It's nice to sit/lie watching, intellect set at nil, the rare luxury of doing sweet nothing. (1985: 21)

> I think it does have substance. Just think of the saying: 'Money can't buy you happiness', you can certainly trace that in *Dallas*. (1985: 105–6)

The importing of programmes like *Dallas* doesn't make Dutch citizens rush to copy the lifestyles of Texan billionaires. They maintain a critical distance from the programme, like many people do when confronted by the vast array of ephemera and white noise that increasingly jostles for people's attention – advertising, clickbait, junk mail. If you don't like it, you don't have to consume it. TVs, smartphones and computers do have an 'off' switch!

Moreover, the 'directions of travel' of cultural products is increasingly difficult to map; global culture isn't simply transmitted from the USA or other members of the global North to a relatively powerless global South. Instead, cultural ideas and products originate from a wide variety of sources. The cultural reach and influence of many nations – sometimes known as their 'soft power' (see Nye, 2005) – can be profound. As Chapter 2 has demonstrated, human society has always interacted with, traded with, and learnt from other cultures and these interactions haven't always been pursued via the conquest and colonization of those cultures. The cultural products of societies different from one's own have often held a deep attraction, as shown since the days of the Silk Road. Today's global communication technologies and international distribution and logistics systems render 'foreign' cultural artefacts more visible and available than ever. Products, philosophies, or practices such as Zen Buddhism, traditional Chinese medicine and Hare Krishna are well established in the global North as parts of an 'alternative' or 'New Age' movement built to some extent around a counter-cultural ethos, attractive to those disaffected and stifled by corporate modernity.

The ways in which McWorld or the Nike swoosh dominate discussions of globalization constructs the 'problem' of global culture in a highly ethnocentric manner which reflects the contemporary dominance of Anglophone academic writing and teaching. It downplays the rather obvious fact that the world has always been a complex universe of varied cultures and civilizations and that human culture, knowledge, technology and science are constructions emanating from across many ethnic traditions, such as the Chinese, Indian, Asian, African or Arabic 'worlds' (Westwood and Jack, 2007). Postcolonial theory teaches that the very notions of 'the West' or 'the global North' are also highly artificial and historically contingent ideological constructs.

And it is not just the 'traditional' elements of non-Western cultures that have a large cultural footprint in the global North. An enormous literature from cultural studies and regional studies (much of it informed by postcolonial and postmodernist discourses) describes the growing global influence of commercial cultural products sourced from beyond the core economies of North America and Europe, especially from Japan, South Korea and China (see Ryoo, 2009; Wang and Yeh,

2005; Yano, 2001). There are now many direct competitors to the Western hegemony of pop culture such as the considerable worldwide influence of film, anime, manga and fashion, from Hello Kitty to *Crouching Tiger, Hidden Dragon*. Other countries that have recently joined the front ranks of economic and political influence, such as Saudi Arabia, Russia or China, are using their growing wealth to invest in their own culture industries with the dual goals of making large financial profits and projecting their 'soft power' globally. The Chinese film industry is expanding rapidly, generously funded by the Chinese government and private investors. 2017 saw the release of *The Great Wall*, an epic war movie that was a China–Hollywood co-production shot entirely in English and funded to the tune of 135 million dollars. In what looks like a commercial move by the production company and its financial backers to hedge their bets and protect their investment, Matt Damon was cast in the lead part, leading to accusations of the 'whitewashing' of Chinese history. When 'going global', non-Western cultural producers will often create hybrid works that amplify themes of local and global in making these kinds of commercial compromises.

This points to ambivalence over the degree to which 'global' audiences are comfortable with unfamiliar overseas cultural products. Pop culture commentator Roland Kelts (2006) explores this uncertainty in his book *Japanamerica* which documents how cultural audiences have, under conditions of global hypermediation, become more sophisticated and cosmopolitan. He provides the example of *Battle of the Planets*, a late 1970s TV cartoon series that was imported to American television networks from Japan. Originally the US TV bosses were sceptical that this highly particular Japanese product would interest American kids and advertising executives. Its Japanese title was *Kagaku ninja-tai Gatchaman* which for starters needed a bit of work! The violence would also need turning down. The programme got a major rework that amounted to cultural censorship; plotlines were made more linear and less melodramatic, nobody died and in came a 'kooky' little robot called 7-Zark-7 that was somewhat reminiscent of a dustbin-shaped android from another major science fiction franchise. *Battle of the Planets* turned out to be a huge success. But Kelts argues that this success took place in spite of, rather than because of, the stylistic changes inserted by the Americans. American TV viewers wanted more of the edgier and more unusual Japanese material. The TV industry soon got braver. Products started to be exported to the States with only minimal cultural editing. Pokémon, Tamagotchi, Power Rangers – the more unfamiliar the better. Kelts' argument emphasizes a progressive improvement in global cultural understanding. Consumers and producers of global pop culture are becoming ever more open to newness, strangeness and hybridity. Social boundaries and expectations that once separated and defined 'culture' are becoming fluid and uncertain.

A similar example of the progressive destabilizing of both 'global' and 'Japanese' culture can be seen in the long-running *Metal Gear* video game franchise. Originating in 1987 on the MSX home computer gaming system that had little take-up outside of Japan, the object of this military-themed game was to operate undetected and sneak past enemies, deliberately avoiding noisy and bloody firefights. The 'stealth' genre was formed, whereby the player aims to fool the enemy by tapping on walls or hiding in cardboard boxes rather than blasting them to bits. While the games were increasingly marketed globally and the main character looked and sounded like some kind of American Green Beret, the 'Japaneseness' of the product always remained deliberately prominent. The plot lines were bizarre and manga-like in their complexity and melodrama and often involved the appearance of fantastical creations. One moment the gamer faces off against Soviet soldiers, the next some weird guy who attacks by controlling swarms of hornets. The writer and director of the games, Hideo Kojima, became a minor celebrity and was feted as the world's first 'postmodern' video game designer. Like *Pokémon* and *Battle of the Planets*, the Japanese 'weirdness' was part of the series' appeal, an alternative to mainstream US flag-waving 'war on terror' type 'shooter' games such as *SOCOM US Navy Seals Fire Team Bravo 3*. The character would eat Japanese noodles to restore energy, wear a samurai headband and battle with *Godzilla*-like 'mechs'. While very violent, the plots carried powerful anti-war messages about nuclear weapons, child soldiers and the war profiteering of private military contractors. Throughout all was a playful sense of pastiche and irony: influences ranged across manga, James Bond, Rambo, spaghetti Westerns, *Dr Strangelove* and cult B-movies such as *Escape from New York*.

As the franchise developed it became progressively globalized in several ways. It remains very much a Japanese product, but it is increasingly a creation of an international workforce of designers and artists. By the late 2000s gaming technology had moved on so much that video games started to outgrow the genre limitations imposed by prior technologies. With *Metal Gear*, this seemed to have the effect of removing some of its Japanese design and appearance. In-game characters' body movements had for some time been motion-captured by electronic sensors placed on the bodies of real people, but by the mid-2010s, even in-game characters' facial expressions would be mapped in this way. The budget and exposure of this franchise expanded and eventually the Hollywood megastar Kiefer Sutherland was booked to play the lead role. Much of the musical score was created by the British producer

Harry Gregson-Williams who has written dozens of scores for Hollywood action movies. Music to accompany the trailers of the newest edition of the game was licensed from Western pop outfits such as New Order and Garbage. Product placement started to creep into the game, such as Triumph motorcycles and *Playboy* magazine. While still a very distinct franchise, one can't help thinking it loses something of its uniqueness as it globalizes, driven both by commercial imperatives and by the growing capacity of gaming hardware. Kelts is right to suggest that the boundaries of foreign and Western cultures are increasingly becoming blurred, but it is equally important to note that these creative relationships are always at the mercy of financial calculations, much like the casting of Matt Damon in *The Great Wall*.

It is also important to consider how the intermixing of cultural tropes and techniques is not simply a result of the direct *importing* of overseas cultures into new hosts. Hybrid cultural forms also emerge from processes of *local emulation and mirroring*, such as the US children's' cartoon *Ben Ten* that copies Japanese animation styles, or the British fashion brand Superdry that does a similar thing with clothes. Multicultural societies can also generate rich new cultural productions, such as the music artist Apache Indian (see Jalan, 1997), a British citizen of Indian descent whose work reflected the varied musical and cultural influences of growing up in ethnically mixed Birmingham in the 1980s. There is a very powerful literary tradition produced by writers who have directly experienced migration and diaspora – see for example the prolific work of Pakistani–British author Meera Syal or the Pulitzer-prize winning novel *The Sympathizer* by Vietnamese–American writer Viet Than Nguyen.

Cultural outputs have always been influenced by transnational sources. Culture will 'ransack the world storehouse' – in the words of Daniel Bell – 'to engorge any and every style it comes upon' (Bell, 1979: 13). This ability to create and distribute hybrid multicultural products is today boosted by the increasing availability of easy-to-use home-made software packages for the reimagining, spoofing and mashing-up of culture and media. The availability of new technology, the rise of content-sharing websites and the deregulation of media and cultural product markets has intensified these processes of cultural mixing, producing new multicultural works that range from highbrow novels to outrageous rip-offs. A notorious example of the latter would be a track entitled *Şımarık* meaning 'naughty' by Turkish pop star Tarkan. It underwent over 25 cover versions recorded by overseas artists in different languages from English to Persian, with the song title changing to, among others, *Kiss Kiss*; *Yek! Na Do Ta;* and *Chiku Chiku Bum Bum*. Alluding to the formation of mixed-heritage languages that developed out of histories of colonialism, migration and diaspora, global culture theorists often use the term 'Creolization' to describe the creation and interplay of new, hybrid cultures and sensibilities (Cohen, 2007).

And this is only to mention cultural products created and distributed by professionals on a commercial basis. YouTube and Vimeo overflow with *homemade* hybrid culture creations: 'Star Wars Gangsta Rap', 'Donald Duck meets Glenn Beck', 'Donald Trump visits Trumpton' – the possibilities are endless. Versions of the phrase 'good artists copy, great artists steal' have been attributed to T.S. Eliot, Igor Stravinsky, Pablo Picasso and Steve Jobs – the rapid increases in the power and sophistication of computer processing and graphic and sonic manipulation, combined with the ubiquity of social media have turned global society into a thief's paradise. Law professor, Lawrence Lessig has argued that the time has come to rethink outdated copyright laws that are unworkable in this riotous new global free-for-all (2008). The *Gaye vs. Thicke* copyright infringement case of 2015 saw a US federal court order pop artist Robin Thicke and his publisher Sony to pay over 7 million dollars in damages to the estate of Marvin Gaye. The decision claimed Thicke had unlawfully copied the 'feel' and 'sound' of Gaye's 1977 track *Got to Give it Up* in their 2013 hit *Blurred Lines*. The contorted legal arguments that decide cases like these seem increasingly arbitrary and potentially highly restrictive of the hybridizing practices of quotation and mimicry associated with global culture.

Countries with less restrictive intellectual property rights legislations make for interesting comparisons. Until recently Turkey, for example, has never fully recognized the international copyright 'rules of the game' as set by transnational organizations such as the WTO. This has allowed the traditions of 'borrowing' or 'tribute making' of cultural products to take on a whole new level. As shown in the highly entertaining documentary movie, *Remake, Remix, Rip-Off* (2014) directed by Cem Kaya and funded by a German regional film board, the Turkish film industry churned out *thousands* of low-budget movies that directly ripped off Western movies' plots, characters, posters and soundtracks, even going as far as splicing in entire film clips. Turkish film included science fiction epics, Westerns, war movies, police thrillers – all at laughably low production standards. It is interesting to reflect on why such a documentary film would be made today. With a global audience that grew up on internet memes, mashups, irony and pastiche it could be that these Turkish films perfectly symbolize the collapse of a Western-imposed cultural order and the WTO-enforced intellectual property rights designed to police it. Turkish 'cowboy' film-makers are portrayed almost as anti-Western visionaries, subversively using the technologies and artefacts of McWorld to unsettle and ridicule American cultural hegemony.

But, as in Chapter 3, we return to the issue of the critique of globalization actually somehow being part of globalization's reproduction and further diffusion. Yes, you are permitted to have a joke at the expense of George Lucas, Rambo or Walt Disney, but in doing so you are really paying homage to the Hollywood gods and their corporate backers. In the UK, an amusing protest took place in December 2009 when a Facebook campaign developed to prevent Joe McEldery – that year's winner of the TV talent-show *X-Factor* – from almost automatically becoming number one in the Christmas pop music chart by virtue of the airplay dominance provided by the TV show. All of a sudden, sales surged for an anarchic and expletive-ridden 1992 track *Killing in the Name* by Los Angeles rock band Rage Against the Machine. Their song beat McEldery's to the number one spot, in what appeared to be a popular strike back against a profit-driven corporate music industry that was systematically destroying creativity with its anodyne, manufactured offerings. But in another example of the circularity of anti-globalization protest this was a Pyrrhic victory; both of these music acts were signed to record labels owned by Sony Corporation!

Today the global culture industry, despite its profits being to some extent threatened by piracy and illegal file sharing, is hardly quaking in its boots when confronted by internet protest campaigns, boycotts, spoofs and rip-off movies. These are pretty insignificant as forms of critique. But, as mentioned in the opening to this chapter, other parts of the global culture debate have a much darker edge than internet campaigns against the *X-Factor* or academic critiques of McDonald's, Disney or *Dallas*. A large part of the globalization literature documents the prevalence of intercultural conflict, violence, xenophobia and racism that, even in the face of cultural imperialism and hybridization, remain as important to the globalization story as ever.

A clash of civilizations? Globalization as grievance, violence and blowback

It is widely taken as a given that globalization has many forms, and that globalization does not simply mean the steady international spread of neoliberal capitalism, Western culture and democracy. Manfred Steger describes three main projections of globalization: market globalism, justice globalism and jihadist globalism (Steger, 2013). The first concept clearly refers to neoliberal global capitalism of the first wave literature. The second refers to the critics of global market capitalism who demand reform to curb its harshest effects on the less powerful members of society (see Chapter 3). 'Jihadist globalism' is somewhat less clear as a concept and there is considerable controversy around the use of the term 'jihad' in globalization studies. An Arabic word for 'struggle' or 'effort', it has been used widely by Western authors such as Benjamin Barber in his 'Jihad versus McWorld' writings (Barber, 1992; 2011) to refer to a vision of globalization based not around markets, competition and democracy in the style of mainstream Western economic globalization, but a form of global integration based on some kind of religious, ethnic, political or cultural ideology – normally one that opposes Western-led market globalization. While the use of the word 'jihad' in Western media is usually made in relation to Islamist extremism or terrorism, this would be only one kind of many possible understandings of tribalism or 'jihad globalism' (see also Steger, 2005; 2013), in which various groups pursue distinctive visions of the global that are based not around Western Enlightenment ideals of 'progress' or liberty, but rather on much more traditional political, ethnic, nationalist or religious aims.

The idea that there are competing visions of a global society is not a new one. The Cold War that dominated the second half of the twentieth century represented a grand ideological battle over whether the ideas and practices of communism or capitalism were the more advanced, the more just, and the more logical in the pursuit of human progress, wealth generation, and political and cultural representation. Both communism and capitalism had their own 'global' visions or 'models' of a rational society which they tried to project around the world while simultaneously attempting to restrict the spread of the other. As discussed in Chapter 1, the collapse of the Soviet Union in 1991 stimulated wide speculation that the communist model of economics and government had utterly failed, meaning that competition over versions of a good society will no longer be primarily economic or political because surely no fool would continue to back the broken and discredited communist system? (Fukuyama, 1992).

For conservative political scientists such as Samuel Huntingdon (1993), international conflict would no longer be played out on the hardened Cold War terrains of economics, political theory or military strategy, but on the shifting and ephemeral sands of culture, identity, ethnicity, nationhood and religion. Rather than the rational world of free markets and liberal democracy championed by the first wave globalization writings, the world would become a messy and violent place characterized by a 'clash of civilizations' (Huntingdon, 1993). This viewpoint was endorsed by those who argued that globalization is unleashing an explosion of violence and a reawakening of 'ancient hatreds' (see Kaplan, 1993). Rather than constructing a New World Order or globalizing pluralist liberal democracy, interethnic wars and insurgencies were being fought out with deadly consequences and little regard for civil society or Bretton Woods-style rules of engagement. These New Wars (Kaldor, 2012) were 'among the people' with high degrees of civilian casualties, often involving unlawful combatants and non-state actors such as militias, gangsters or even child soldiers. Atrocities such as 'ethnic cleansing' and mass executions were disturbingly commonplace. 24/7 news media accentuated certain place-names as they became bywords for atrocities. To a 'global' media, hitherto unheard-of locales came to be defined by violence and tragedy: Nagorno-Karabakh, Grozny, Rwanda, Srebrenica. TV audiences of the global North were often oblivious to these wars, and struggled to comprehend their causes and motives. The Second Congo War or Great Africa War of 1998–2003 involved the military forces of nine African countries alongside maybe 20 other armed groups. The nation once known as Zaire was ripped asunder. Estimates of the death toll (much of it due to disease and starvation) ranged between 4 and 7 million people. US and Western powers agonized over whether or not to intervene in these complex and brutal conflicts. If the root causes of the violence were 'cultural', 'tribal' and 'irrational', then what good would intervention do?

Predictions made in the first wave globalization literature about the spread of peace, stability and wealth seemed hopelessly unrealistic: 'We hoped for order. We got pandemonium' (Ignatieff, 1994: 28). Global security think tanks speculated about a new 'chaos theory' that might better explain the harsh realities of globalization than a New World Order or an End of History. Epidemiologists calculated that as many as 5.4 million people had died of war and violence-related injuries from 1955–2002, with no evidence of any recent decline in death rates (Obermeyer et al., 2008). Journalists joined the fray with a range of depressing writings which characterize globalization as wretched poverty, widespread resentment and bloody violence, such as Perry's (2008) *Falling off the Edge*. Some were sceptical of such a dystopian view. Sadowski in *The Myth of Global Chaos* (1998) argues that the nature of inter-group conflicts and grievances have not really changed over centuries and that the Huntingdon doomsday scenario of globalization triggering increasing cultural violence is inaccurate.

But the rise of religious extremism, the 9/11 attacks and the global war on terror seemed to connect rather too well with Huntingdon and Barber's doom-mongering. The 'clash of civilizations' and Jihad vs. McWorld paradigms seemed to neatly capture the intensity of these new 'culture wars' in which logic and rationality don't seem to apply.

When the Taliban group took control of Afghanistan in the mid to late 1990s, culture, behaviour and dress were tightly controlled on pain of death. Cinemas, TVs, VCRs and music were banned outright, as were nail polish, wine and sewing catalogues. 'Throw reason to the dogs' read a sign posted to the wall of the Taliban religious police (Wright, 2006: 231). But the paradoxes of globalization meant that extremist violence seemed to be accelerated and enabled by the cultural, scientific and technological products of the very same global society that extremists wanted to destroy. Academics writing in the disciplines of international politics or security studies often argue that extremist jihad is a global phenomenon, describing the international spread of specific tactics such as suicide terrorism being common among 'network based' extremist groups (see Pedhazur and Perliger, 2006). As we will explore in the next chapter, the notion of a 'network' is widely asserted as the most effective and logical organizational form in an age of globalization.

The grand strategy of Islamist terror appeared to be one of luring the US and its allies into large-scale military responses such as the invasions of Afghanistan and Iraq, tying them down in counterinsurgency quagmires that they cannot escape from and creating further grievances as American and European powers unleash their violence on Arabs and Muslims (Hill, 2008: 12–14). According to Joseph Stiglitz, the former World Bank chief economist and a leading proponent of 'justice globalism', the 'Iraq war has contributed to a "clash of civilizations", a perception that there is a new crusade against Islam.' He claims that the American-led invasion has 'intensified feelings of animosity which are likely to be a source of conflict for years in the future' (Stiglitz and Bilmes, 2008: 144).

Years of indeterminate conflict in Iraq and the civil war in neighbouring Syria opened up a lawless space for the emergence of a so-called Islamic Caliphate, known variously as ISIL, ISIS or Daesh; a new non-state actor that has declared itself the authentic geographic focal-point for global Islamist extremism. Burnt by the failures, costs and blowback of the wars in Iraq and Afghanistan, and cautious of a resurgent Russia's complex ties to the Middle East, Western powers are extremely wary of engaging in large-scale ground operations to confront ISIL. The US-led 'war on terror' downshifted from regular contact with the enemy to a remote form of 'drone theory', as brilliantly theorized by Chamayou (2015). The bloody business of war has been computerized and semi-automated. Violence has been rendered remote, sanitized and 'risk free', at least to combatants representing the global North. But drone attacks do little to create the stability or security demanded by the North's militaries. Although far less risky and costly than putting boots on the ground, drone wars threaten to drag on indefinitely. Drones and their broader operational systems and risk calculi make for threat-reduced conditions but cannot conjure up victory scenarios. The US and its allies are condemned to fight never-ending wars and face never-ending blowback. Strategists in the Pentagon work up a 'Prompt Global Strike' program, with the aim of delivering a 'lethal package' of precision-guided munitions to any territory in the world within one hour. Such is the 'striking militarization of globalization' (Scholte, 2005: xiii). But the more the US extends itself, the more blowback it can expect to receive (Johnson, 2002). Similar fates possibly await other ambitious major powers such as China and Russia.

If peace and security really are the goals of the world's great powers then perhaps more thought needs to go into the prevention of grievances that encourage violence and conflict. It is almost a cliché that France is largely hostile to American-led globalization (Veseth, 2010: 157–79). French philosopher Alain Badiou (2016) in *Our Wound is Not So Recent*, argues that the processes of globalization are deeply complicit with an upsurge in chaos and violence. Discussing the recent terror attacks on France, Badiou argues that extremist violence is not simply meaningless and wilful killing carried out by brainwashed zealots. For Badiou it is the by-product of economic and political exclusion in which increasing parts of the world's population find themselves in 'ungovernable zones' of precarity and incivility. This is a position that more mainstream commentators will occasionally mention but never fully commit to as it would put them in the uncomfortable position of admitting that in certain cases 'jihadist' grievances are understandable. By Badiou's logic 'jihad globalism' might intersect to some degree with 'justice globalization'. Fragments of this troublesome line of argument are visible in the 9/11 Commission's report when it proclaims that the West's confrontation with global terrorism cannot be exclusively pursued in the military realm. Just as in the titanic ideological battle of the Cold War, the ideational attraction of nationalist, ethnic or religious extremism must also be countered by the US and its allies. The 9/11 Commission argued that extremist ideology 'appeals to people disoriented by cyclonic change as they confront modernity and globalization' (9/11 Commission, 2004: 48). People may become radicalized by the internet rantings of dangerous ideologues, but why might they be prepared to log in and listen in the first place? Perhaps because their lives are meaningless and hard. Journalist Lawrence Wright argues that the doctrines and practices of Islamist extremism reverse the essentially peaceful and harmonious teachings of the Muslim faith (2006: 124). In *The Looming Tower* (2006) he documents the contexts of lawlessness, unemployment and hopelessness where poisonous ideologies might thrive: '[a]nger, resentment, and humiliation spurred young Arabs to search for dramatic remedies' (2006: 107).

The same, of course, is true of other 'hate' groups such as white supremacists, nationalists, or neo-Nazis. Diatribes by the British Nationalist Party or the English Defence League describe decades of 'attacks' on 'the English race' or 'the white race'. Poisonous racist ideology is promoted internationally on neo-Nazi websites such as 'Stormfront'. Hate groups on social media are important examples of a deluded and ugly identity politics based on the purported grievances that are claimed to flow from globalization. Paradoxically, extreme nationalists have to some extent also 'gone global': skinheads in Italy or South Africa link up with racists in Britain to mutually complain about how their nations and 'races' are being swamped by immigrants, distorted by multiculturalism or forcibly governed by Sharia Law or Zionism. Extreme right-wingers also increasingly demonize Islam, creating a cycle whereby opposing extremist movements feed off one another (Eatwell and Goodwin, 2010: 7). Racist and homophobic fanatics develop and promulgate an unworkable and rather pathetic politics of blame and hatred that seems unlikely to be successful as it rarely finds broad support.

This is a central, if often unacknowledged, point in the literature on global culture wars – extremists are at the fringes of society and their destructive rhetoric is repulsive to the overwhelming majority of citizens. This is attested to by the track record of failure of extremist politics in democratic elections despite the extensive and excited media coverage these groups often enjoy. Rather than the age of globalization creating more hatred, fear and xenophobia by placing different people into closer proximity, there is considerable evidence to suggest that globalization is actually associated with greater intercultural tolerance. Put simply, one might reasonably assume that every human being tends to want the same basic things: a peaceful life and a roof over their heads for themselves and their families, a degree of wealth and security. The growth of migration and multiculturalism means a more widespread experience of living side-by-side with those of other cultural and ethnic backgrounds. It is perhaps reasonable to hope that over time this leads to a reduction in xenophobia and racism as familiarity grows and older prejudices are challenged (Back et al., 2001; Easton, 2014).

Some important thinkers have claimed that violence and crime is actually in decline, and that the scale of war deaths are grossly exaggerated (Bregman, 2016: 19–20; Pinker, 2011: 384). Globalization might thus lead to *less* violence, not more, as more of the world eventually comes to experience the economic growth and rule of law that global markets and liberal democracy are supposed to provide. Culture wars associated with globalization are surely nowhere near as violent and sustained when compared to religious and ethnic wars of earlier periods of history such as the Crusades. The prospects of being embroiled in a terrorist incident, becoming a victim of a racist hate crime, or waking up to find a neo-Nazi party elected are fairly remote. Even so, however, the baleful influences of these globalizing hate groups are real. The danger lies less with their (limited) electoral prospects but with their potential ability to influence political and cultural discourses. Ambitious and unscrupulous politicians pinpoint and magnify feelings of resentment and grievance, with populists like Donald Trump – 'a rancorous Twitter troll' (Mishra, 2016) – elected to the US Presidency by harvesting the rhetoric sown by these ill winds.

This final point sets up the discussions of the following chapter. Trump was a total outsider in the 2016 Presidential race, with many observers saying he profited by ripping up the political rule book. Compared to his Democratic Party challenger Hillary Clinton he had no 'ground game': he had far fewer local offices and volunteers to go door-knocking and to 'get out the vote'. He never had the full backing of the Republican Party either. He went 'straight for the gut', making outrageous claims on Twitter or Breitbart News and holding rallies in convention centres and sports arenas. He wasn't interested in the expert views and tactics of established think tanks or pollsters. Ever the salesman, he focused his energies on the direct marketing of Brand Trump, cutting out the 'middlemen' of established political organizations in his unlikely path to the White House (Klein, 2017). His campaign represented a new form of organization, highly attuned to today's globalized, digitized, hypermediated and deeply uncertain environment. Globalization is often associated with new forms of organization: everywhere in the global literature we see reference to the power of lean, innovative and non-hierarchical companies based around the virtuality of the internet and social media. Fears abound about global 'networks' of terrorism. The 9/11 Commission report promotes new ways to organize government in order to respond to the new global conditions of risk and insecurity; less hierarchy, less centralization, more rapid decision-making, more sharing of information. The following chapter will explore these organizational debates in depth as we explore how globalization encourages organizations of all kinds (multinational corporations; government agencies; think tanks and civil society groups; military and law enforcement) to change the way they do business in order to survive and prosper in an increasingly complex, fast-moving, confusing and interconnected globalized society.

5

Global Times, Global Organizations?

The uptake of communications devices in mainstream jobs has brought a conclusive end to utopian dreams that the Internet will revolutionize the working day.

(Gregg, 2011: 16)

The waking lives of millions of people around the world are dominated by the experiences of work. Years are set by the rhythms, artefacts and locations of labour: the hum of office air conditioning units, the non-stop ping of emails, phone calls, meetings, spreadsheets, performance management 'dashboards', construction sites, logistics centres, cold and lonely railway stations and roadside cafes. Globalization is supposed to reach into and transform every aspect of human life. Its impact on organizations, management and work is potentially huge. The expansion of global markets implies significant disruption to the ways in which corporations are structured and how they operate. Managers working in almost any line of business will tell you that global competition is tougher than it has ever been. Global markets mean increased pressure on all companies to perform well or risk bankruptcy. New technologies are brought to market ever faster, making hitherto successful businesses obsolete and intensifying the pressure for companies to offer products and services that can beat the competition on quality and cost.

Globalization also provides companies with new opportunities. Companies adopt a 'global sourcing' model, making use of transnational production networks or 'value chains' (Sturgeon, 2002). They can hire staff from potentially anywhere in the world, seeking out cheaper or better-qualified employees from global rather than national or local labour markets. Large multinationals generate complex webs of subsidiary organizations across various jurisdictions and funnel their incomes through offshore territories and 'shell' entities to limit their exposure to taxation (Fichtner, 2014). The pressures, risks and incentives of global financial markets operate in 'real time' with senior managers paying close attention to the behaviour of stocks, bonds, currencies and interest rates across various international financial markets (Holton, 2012).

Globalization also implies changes to the internal workings of organizations. Writings on globalization and organization assert that the basic principles of management, work and employment have been fundamentally challenged by the rise of our global age. The classical organizational form of the twentieth century – the bureaucratic hierarchy – is widely regarded as ineffective in globalized times. Global fluidity and connectedness have made traditional organizational forms hopelessly outdated. Old-line pyramid-shaped hierarchies channelled authority and decision-making to the summit of the organization, while middle managers, supervisors and front line workers followed standard operating procedures. Such an old-fashioned 'Fordist' model is often said to be obsolete in the age of globalization – it is too slow, cumbersome, inflexible and unresponsive. Globalization implies constant change, movement and instability. It therefore both enables and perhaps requires commercial and public organizations to redesign themselves in the direction of flexible networks rather than rigid hierarchies.

This chapter will address the various ways in which globalization interacts with organization. It begins by describing why so many globalization and business writers declare and often celebrate the obsolescence of Fordist models of organization, and will explore the validity of claims that these old-fashioned hierarchies are being replaced with 'networks' as the organizing principle in globalized times. Throughout, the chapter is not solely concerned with corporations and commerce; the impacts and processes of globalization seem to affect all manner of organizations including government agencies, social movements, criminal or terrorist groups, even of anti-globalization protest movements. Once again the chapter portrays globalization as a seemingly inescapable and ever-present condition or 'syndrome' (Mittelman, 2000), often with paradoxical symptoms, such as alter-globalization or anti-capitalist movements mirroring the new organizational forms and the philosophies of the global corporations that they hold in disdain.

From pyramids to spider webs: Globalization's threat to bureaucracy

As we saw in Chapter 2, capitalism arguably started to really globalize in the early twentieth century (although not without crises and reversals along the way). Several developments in the 1920s bonded nations and their economies closer together in the period between the disasters of the First World War and the Wall Street Crash. Interest groups developed that aimed to broaden and deepen international collaboration. One of these was the International Committee for Scientific Management, a group of scholars which promoted what purported to be rational, scientific, standardized and efficient approaches to organization that should replace the ad hoc, traditional, and very varied managerial and industrial practices in common usage. Writings on industrial efficiency by American and European writers circulated the newsletters and conferences of what amounted to an international management movement (Brech et al., 2010). Classical British management writer Lyndall Urwick recalled a meeting in Paris in 1929 where he met a Lithuanian–American scholar named V.A. Graicunas who believed he'd discovered a mathematic formula for calculating the most efficient managerial hierarchy that could apply to any organization (Urwick, 1974). Graicunas claimed that organizations cannot be expected to work efficiently with a span of control broader than five – in other words, no manager can really cope with having to supervise more than five direct reports. Organizations should have narrow spans of control and tall hierarchies, allowing tight supervision of staff at all levels. Substantial numbers of managers would be employed in mid-level positions spread up and down many layers of middle management. Such a structure would imply potentially long careers inside one company. There'd be an internal career ladder where managers could climb the hierarchy over time, much like an officer in the military, or a civil servant in a government ministry. Many of these classical management theorists had direct experience of military and/or government service and these cultures of operation are imprinted on their writings (Urwick, 1974). The most efficient and modern organization structure was visualized as a pyramid. Rules were rules. Only minimal authority or discretion was devolved downwards.

Such management thinking became widespread in the industrialized world during most of the twentieth century. Large organizations were tightly controlled by bureaucratic systems of rules, plans, targets, procedures, committees, manuals and documents. Technological developments initially complemented this approach, with early computer systems in the 1960s tending to re-enforce Fordist principles of standardization, economies of scale, and the strict measurement and recording of activity via bureaucratic metrics and information systems. Many of the processes and principles of logistics, accounting and operations were derived from the field known as 'operations research' that was developed and applied by government and military organizations in the Second World War (Waring, 1991).

After the war, these modes of operation and their associated managerial structures were central to the running of large business and government organizations of the 'golden age' of capitalist expansion. The emphasis was on stability. A well-managed company follows routines, sets plans and measures progress. The pyramid-shaped organization would be partitioned into clear divisions in which everyone knew their place and duty: Operations, Personnel, Accounts, Marketing. This bureaucratic approach seemed to work well in the 1950s and 1960s when economies were growing relatively rapidly year-on-year and when international competition had yet to fully develop. Many countries developed national economic plans and industrial strategies. Substantial parts of a country's industry and banking were nationalized and commercial firms were often closely supported by government and known as 'national champions'. A shorthand academic term for this economic model was 'Fordism' which refers both to the centralized management principles of organizations and to the broader political structure of a nation's economy.

However, as global economic integration really accelerated in the 1980s and 1990s, Fordism became problematic. Global market competition, the rise of services sectors (knowledge industries, financial industries, culture industries), the reduction of international tariff barriers, and the explosive proliferation of new information technologies created entirely new ways of thinking about management structures and economic policy. Notions of a bounded, national economy underpinned by traditional bureaucratic organizational structures were obsolete. Fordism gave way to 'post-Fordism' (Amin, 1994) and ultimately to a post-industrial economy increasingly dominated by services and especially finance. Volume manufacturing in the advanced economies largely collapsed as factories were closed and industrial assembly moved to subcontracted overseas operators (Adler, 2000; Broughton, 2015).

Crisis and confusion seemed to swirl around the established Western European or North American economies as they suddenly struggled with the intense competition provided by rising Asian powers. Management as a profession was also attacked. In a famous article published in the *Harvard Business Review*, Robert Hayes and William Abernathy claimed that US companies were 'managing [their] way to economic decline'; companies were micromanaged, too bureaucratic, not sufficiently creative or innovate, and just too slow to keep up with global competition (Hayes and Abernathy, 1980). Caught in a blizzard of pointless, self-generated paperwork and obsessed with trying to quantify and measure every last detail, companies had lost sight of the essence and purpose of what they were supposed to be doing. The new global marketplace, according to management guru Tom Peters, 'is demanding that we burn the policy manuals and knock off the incessant memo-writing; there just isn't time for it' (Peters, 1992: xv). It was time to reform traditional corporate structures: throw out the rule book, flatten the hierarchy and downsize the mid-level pen-pushers. Images of an agile, streamlined, post-bureaucratic and less tightly controlled organizational form were attractive both to the dynamic chief executive keen to stir things up and make an impact as well as the disaffected cubical drone further down the pecking order who can't handle another week of shuffling paperwork or another afternoon sat in some tedious committee meeting.

Basic organizing principles of management were rhetorically over-turned, with globalization as the driving impulse. The globalization of business education and publishing and the ubiquity of the English lan-guage served to diffuse new 'best practice' management models rapidly and widely around the world (McCann, 2016). The vogue for organi-zational form changed drastically from the 1980s onwards. The metaphor of the pyramid was replaced with that of the spider web. Companies cannot be meaningfully understood as self-contained hier-archical structures in which all workers operate according to strict, top-down command and control and are located in separate depart-ments by function. Instead, organizations affected by (and contributing to) the processes of globalization need to be reconstituted as flexible, contingent, temporary and fluid structures that are loosely bound in complex networks of association (Castells, 2000; Reich, 1991). The tech-stock boom of the 1990s saw the rapid development of entrepre-neurial companies; small in size, focused, with flat organizational structures and funded by venture capital.

Companies today create complex webs of suppliers, distributors, subcontractors and financiers. The imperatives of global financial mar-kets force firms to shut down, spin off, or outsource non-core parts of their business. Back-office functions such as IT or payroll are out-sourced to shared services centres which could be located in another country thousands of miles away (McCann, 2014b). Walls between staff are eroded by the impetus towards temporary project work that cuts across divisional boundaries. Core workers are kept on and given more responsibility and pay while a periphery of others are made redundant or replaced by 'flexible' or self-employed contractors. Organizations become 'virtual' (Thorne, 2005). Assets are shared among many different entities. Products and services are co-produced by multiple designers, suppliers, assemblers and distributors across many different firms and suppliers. Equipment and real estate are leased from third parties. New digital management information systems replace the bureaucratic ranks of middle managers and clerks who are no longer needed. Organizational hierarchies are flattened as email, smartphones and social media platforms enable spans of control to become far broader than the classical theorists thought possible. Micromanaging goes out of style to be replaced with more flexible forms of 'leadership' that supposedly allow the downward devolution of operating discretion.

Instead of a cumbersome, bureaucratic pyramid that aims to provide a stability that is unworkable and self-defeating, the organization as web or network suddenly appears as the most appropriate organizational shape for the turmoil and flux of globalization. The position is summarized here by the former US Secretary of Labor, Robert Reich:

> The high-value enterprise has no need to control vast resources, discipline armies of production workers or impose predictable routines. Thus it need not be organized like the old pyramids that characterized standardized production, with strong chief executives presiding over ever-widening layers of managers, atop an even larger group of hourly workers, all following standard operating procedures. In fact, the high-value enterprise *cannot* be organized this way. [...] There is no place for bureaucracy. (Reich, 1991: 87)

The organization as network is in keeping with the computerized, digitized, information-rich, fast-moving and geographically dispersed nature of globalization. A slimmed-down, focused, de-bureaucratized and networked organization might simply be a more efficient way of operating that has logically and virtuously spread far and wide (Castells, 2000; Reich, 1991). The global, networked organization is innovative, agile and flexible; it's able to harness the creativity of its committed employees rather than just ordering them about. However, as we shall see below, the concepts, philosophies and operating practicalities of networks and webs are also associated with a wide range of problems.

Networks, webs and chains: Liberation or incarceration?

The rhetoric of replacing bureaucracy with networks bonds seamlessly with mainstream literature that promotes globalization as inevitable, efficient, modern and progressive. No-one wants to be employed by an organization that runs in a top-down manner and bores its workers to death with paperwork and repetitive routines. Industrial jobs have declined, but who'd want to carry out the dangerous and monotonous work of a steel mill or a car factory? We all want instead to work in cultural and knowledge industries, wandering around open-plan offices in smart suits, flicking our fingers across tablets, coming up with innovative social media strategies before chilling out for a bit on the beanbags. Don't we?

The globalization literature borrows heavily from predictions that started to emerge in the 1970s about a 'post-industrial society' (Bell, 1976). Globalist writers tend to take it as given that work in the global age is increasingly about white-collar, self-directed, creative experts who are independent contractors rather than company lifers. Reich's description of 'symbolic analysts' (1991) or Florida's discussion of a new 'creative class' (2012) are certainly attractive. A global knowledge economy increasingly values those who work in highly paid, involving, discretionary, knowledge-intensive and creative roles that have abstract problem-solving at their core. The skills and attitudes required by such jobs are what schools and universities supposedly need to train young people to embody so that advanced economies are best prepared for a globalized future (Friedman, 2007: 308–36). Florida (2012: vii) claims that the 'creative class' makes up nearly one third of the US workforce.

Frankly that is very hard to believe. Other sources suggest that the globalized service economy creates an enormous amount of low-paid, uncreative, insecure, dead-end jobs. That's on top of more than 30 years of job destruction in the agriculture and manufacturing sectors (Perrucci and Perrucci, 2008; Srnicek and Williams, 2016). The fastest-growing employment sectors over the last 20 years or so are not ones which employ large numbers of knowledge workers. Recently the top ten occupations with the strongest job growth in the USA have been: registered nurse, retail salesperson, home health and personal care assistant, general office clerk, food preparation and service, customer service representative and truck driver (Lockard and Wolf, 2012). Not much there in the way of symbolic analysts or the creative class. Similar patterns have prevailed in other post-industrial societies.

Many of the jobs created by the globalized service economy are 'McJobs' (Ritzer, 2014; 115–31): poorly-paid, deskilled, lacking career headroom and subject to very tight managerial control (Frayne, 2015). While jobs in the steel mill or refrigerator factory might have been physically exhausting and possibly hazardous, it paid a lot better and possibly had more intrinsic interest than pressing buttons on an espresso machine all afternoon, wishing customers a nice day through gritted teeth, or sweeping crusty French fries off the kitchen floor at two in the morning. Nearly one million workers in Britain are currently employed on 'zero-hours' contracts (Reuben, 2016), meaning they face daily insecurity about whether or not they can afford to pay their bills or arrange childcare. Retail outlets, restaurants, hotels and care homes are among the widest users of such employment conditions, in keeping with the growth in those sectors. New information systems and software such as smartphone apps have enabled the development of the so-called 'gig economy' or 'sharing economy', where people 'log on' to work via a digital system, work for a few hours if there is demand, then log off. Companies such as Deliveroo and Uber have pioneered such systems, undercutting the competition by limiting their costs and liabilities by claiming they don't employ anyone. Instead they simply claim to provide a software platform that independent operators may find useful. The gig economy is potentially highly exploitative. The remote nature of the working relationship makes it hard for unions to organize workers or governments to regulate the employment relationship. The processes of job creation and job destruction seem to be another way in which globalization extends and intensifies social, economic and regional inequality. So desperate are some people to get a shot at highly paid, involving work they will work for free as interns for months on end. Not everyone has the abilities to be a knowledge worker and not enough knowledge work is being created to employ all the people who do.

New technologies are often championed as one of the main driving forces of restructured, globalized workplaces (Castells, 2000). But, as with Uber's smartphone app, digital and communication technologies can be double-edged in their effects. Some forms of technology can help to increase efficiency, remove bureaucratic waste, increase worker discretion and connect people of common cause. Others allow employees to cut costs, increase work strain or encourage work addiction and the feeling of being 'always on' (Gregg, 2011; Turkle, 2011: 151–70). Digital technology enables tighter forms of organizational control such as electronic performance management systems that closely monitor workers' efforts and remove discretion and autonomy.

> [T]he information circulating within digital society is too much: too fast, too intense, too thick and complex for individuals or groups to elaborate it consciously, critically, reasonably, with the necessary time to make a decision. Therefore the decision is left to automatisms. (Berardi, 2009: 195)

Even for employees lucky enough to be employed in a 'knowledge-intensive firm' working life is often far from the land of milk and honey portrayed by Florida and others (Srnicek and Williams, 2016). People working in downsized, restructured and networked white-collar workplaces often describe precarious employment conditions, intensified workloads and constant stress (Gregg, 2011; Hassard et al., 2009). Dedicated professionals can be treated with hostility and contempt by senior leaders, for example by being issued with 'at risk of redundancy' notices by email, totally out of the blue. Professionals and mid-level managers who have survived job cuts experience much wider spans of control than before, meaning that work tasks and work problems can come in from anywhere, any time. Email inboxes and key performance indicator 'dashboards' can be horrifying to behold. De-layering was meant to get rid of organizational muffling and allow employees to work together more closely, but the removal of ranks has made people too busy to connect. You can go months without seeing a boss or a mentor, leading to workers feeling isolated, unrecognized and unable to seek advice. Narratives of informality, flexibility and throwing out the rule book are central to 'leadership' discourses, but they run the risk of encouraging senior management to be dismissive of protocol and potentially abuse their positions. Tony Blair's notorious 'sofa' style of government was a good example. It was impossible to know how decisions were made and little was formally committed to writing, raising deep questions about accountability.

Almost inevitably stress, anxiety, burnout and feelings of meaningless and low self-worth are extremely common phenomena in the supposedly 'creative' globalized workplace (Frayne, 2015; Turkle, 2011). New technologies can worsen these problems: smartphones mean that email is checked at evenings, weekends, while looking after the kids or while supposedly on holiday (Gregg, 2011; Noys, 2013: 11). 'Creative' companies that cultivate a self-consciously 'countercultural' image such as Netflix and the Virgin Group now claim they no longer monitor staff vacation time and encourage their workers to take as much holiday as they want (Branson, 2014: 216–18). If the 'creative class' is never off the clock then an open holiday policy imposes no risks or costs on their employers. Some colloquially refer to the Blackberry smartphone as the 'Crackberry' as its usage can be addictive and damaging to health, causing many to now undertake a regular 'digital detox'. Sherry Turkle in *Alone Together* (2011) critiques not only the intensifying and distracting nature of new IT systems, but also the pressures social media places on people to promote, tend and defend their online selves. Developing 'a personal brand' is not just a private hobby. It is increasingly an imperative imposed on workers by their employers and by competitive global capitalism.

Promoting progress means that we are always behind: on high-speed internet, on our Facebook profile, on our email inbox. There are always updates to be made; we are the objects of daily masochism and under constant tension. (Virilio, 2012a: 47)

Working time becomes a new marker of inequality. White-collar workers work 60-plus hours per week grappling with poorly designed IT systems and despairing at their overflowing inboxes, while others have nothing, 'hustling' on the streets or sat at home on zero-hours contracts waiting for the phone to ring to offer a few hours on poverty wages. 'We encounter a capitalism that is sometimes quite happy to refuse us work while, at other times, to place extreme demands on us for work' (Noys, 2013: 99).

Despite the ubiquity of dystopian characterizations of employment and unemployment (Berardi, 2009; Frayne, 2015; Srnicek and Williams, 2016), still we are bombarded by excited writings about a brave new world of meaningful, connected, creative and efficient work. Media outlets publish paid-for content about the wonders of the new digital economy; stupid newspaper pull-out sections advocate agility, excitement and meaning at work, plug yet another new social media platform or advertise 'digital skills academies'. One questionable news story described a town in Spain that supposedly decided to get rid of its public services bureaucracy and instead use Twitter for all its administration (Kiss, 2015). Readers' comments added a dose of much-needed realism: 'What a fucking stupid idea' said 'LetThemSnortCoke'.

The global digital economy creates and recycles a Junkspace of cultural ephemera (Koolhaas, 2002), largely on the back of free or near-free labour. Users produce the content, build the brand and spread the word. Social media chatter boosts marketing targets somewhere and generates wealth to be syphoned by the marketers, sponsors and hedge funds who set up and run the platform infrastructure:

> One of the curious aspects of the Twenty-First Century was the great delusion amongst many people, particularly in the San Francisco Bay Area, that *freedom of speech and freedom of expression* were best exercised on technological platforms owned by corporations dedicated to making as much money as possible. (Kobek, 2016: 63)

While a lucky few make millions from a Snapchat or a Tumblr, the rest of us waste time on social media while trying to avoid opening work emails for fear of finding yet another meaningless management update or some spreadsheet of crappy numbers. Promises of the liberation of work through digital networks have turned out to be hollow fantasies (Thorne, 2005).

Global networks of terror, crime and resistance

Networked organizational structures, new global technologies and social media have also been enthusiastically adopted by the opponents of globalization and neoliberalism, by those on the receiving end of downsizing and struggling with the meaninglessness of what LSE anthropology professor David Graeber calls 'bullshit jobs' (Graeber, 2013). He published that particular article in a journal called *Strike!* which advertises itself as a platform for 'grassroots resistance, anti-oppression politics and the philosophies and creative expressions surrounding these movements'. The non-hierarchical, consensual, digitally enabled network is often promoted as the paradigmatic organizing principle for anarchist-inspired protest movements such as Occupy, Argentinian workers' cooperatives, WikiLeaks and countless other critical internet fora. The non-hierarchical philosophy of anarchism is strangely in-tune with the proclamations of business gurus in its desire to reduce 'bureaucracy' and devolve power to the bottom of the organization:

> Crucial to Occupy's globality was its Internet-based diffusion. Like most collective action in recent years, Occupy was highly mediated through a range of online forums, social networks and open-source software and practices. Facebook, Blogs and Twitter were extensively used and many Occupy camps were extremely media savvy. [...] In many ways, this open source or 'free culture, free commons' networking approach mirrors the non-hierarchical organisational structure of the Occupy movement. (Pickerill and Krinsky, 2015: 6–7)

Activist networks, we're told, should have no hierarchy or power structure (Chomsky, 2013). Smash the system. Break the bureaucracy. Once again, we see the paradoxical, almost inescapable nature of globalization; alter-globalization or anti-corporate activists are using the very same concepts, organizational philosophies and technologies that they are hostile to. In some senses, their existence and influence is enabled by and contributes to globalization (Munro, 2015). They are maybe more of a symptom than a cure.

There is also a more sinister element to networks that keeps cropping up in globalization writings. Many have noted that the dispersed, digitally connected network is the most efficient organizational principle not just for global business corporations but also for global terrorist and criminal organizations. Friedman's *The World is Flat* concludes with a discussion of Islamist terror organizations:

> Networks like al-Qaeda use the Internet – not only for easy, cheap, global command and control, but even more important, as a global megaphone to radiate ideas. Indeed some Islamist radical movements have no real command and control [...]. They simply disseminate their ideas globally, using the flat-world platform, and inspire and exhort people to use their local capacity to take initiatives. (Friedman, 2007: 598)

The alleged mastermind of the 9/11 attacks Khalid Sheikh Mohammed was said to have 'pitched' the concept of 'the planes operation' to Osama bin Laden. According to the 9/11 Commission (2004: 154) 'KSM presents himself as an entrepreneur seeking venture capital and people.' The Commission wryly observed that the terrorist planners and operatives 'were more globalized than we were' (2004: 34). The flexible, informal and spontaneous network is the dominant organizational frame of reference for terror, war and crime. Tony Giddens, in *Beyond Left and Right*, suggests a networked structure is necessary for counter-terrorism operations, all enabled and necessitated by highly familiar globalization imperatives:

> [...] militarism [...] was characterized by large-scale, hierarchical systems of command which paralleled the industrial and state bureaucracies. [...] Militarism has declined as a result of several trends: the shifting, and in some ways diminishing, autonomy of nation-states; the disappearance of clear-cut external enemies; the reduced influence of classical nationalism and the rise of substate nationalisms; and the functional obsolescence of large-scale war. (Giddens, 1994a: 233)

I would not be so confident in asserting that militarism has declined in the way that Giddens implies. His rhetoric here is very reminiscent of Kaldor's 'New Wars' thesis, sharing the liberal cosmopolitanism of other 'global civil society' writers such as Held and McGrew (2007) as well as the organizational rhetoric of mainstream business and management gurus. But he is probably right to argue that large-scale war between nations' uniformed armed forces is becoming increasingly unusual (Kaldor, 2012; Pinker, 2011). More common are the complicated New Wars or 'small wars', often involving non-state actors such as terrorist groups and private military contractors. While the richest nations such as the USA and Western European powers sometimes involve themselves in these wars for various reasons, such conflicts are unlikely to directly threaten Western countries' populations or sovereignty, unlike the 'total wars' of the first half of the twentieth century. Security threats to the economically advanced nations are most likely to be associated with 'network-based' violence such as terrorism or cyberattacks.

Network structures are similarly well-represented in discussions of global crime. Law enforcement agencies describe a pandemic of internet fraud. All of us are wearily familiar with identity theft, phishing scams, junk email and unsolicited calls from automated diallers. But beneath the surface of the internet that many of us use every day lies some lesser-known digital realms. These include the 'deep web' of virtual locations that don't feature on search engines and a more sinister 'dark web' that can be accessed only by persons with working knowledge of encryption systems such as 'tors' – software that hides IP addresses and allows internet users to become untraceable by directing traffic through a volunteer network of thousands of relays. The dark web is totally unregulated and parts of it are said to be awash with trade in illegal products and services such as obscene materials, the selling of hacking services, or trade in narcotics and weaponry. The so-called Silk Road was particularly notorious for the online drug trade and was eventually closed by the FBI and Europol in 2013–14.

The organizational principle of a web or network can provide powerful ways to make surreptitious connections while shielding online users and activities from prying eyes. In the rare occasions where networks are compromised and linkages revealed, the world suddenly gets a glimpse of the extent and nature of these private, clandestine and often illicit connections. The 'Panama Papers' was a batch of over 11 million documents extracted from Panamanian law firm Mossack Fonseca and leaked online in 2015, which showed corporations and individuals benefitting from the construction of enormous webs of tax havens and offshore entities which were used to hide assets from tax authorities. Similar revelations appeared in the 'Luxembourg Leaks' of 2014, in which former PriceWaterhouseCoopers employees risked their livelihoods and liberty in blowing the whistle on the complicity of the 'Big Four' auditing firms (Deloitte, Ernst & Young, KPMG, and PwC) in setting up arcane financial connections through the low-tax jurisdiction of Luxembourg that allowed a series of major companies to avoid tax liabilities. One of the whistleblowers, Antoine Deltour, claimed he 'progressively discovered the reality of the system. [...] I didn't want to contribute to that' (as quoted in Marlowe, 2014).

The fluidity and secrecy of network ties makes them difficult for government authorities to counter or expose. Law enforcement and security services, confronted by the global networks of international crime and terrorism, have sometimes tried to 'fight fire with fire' by ditching traditional bureaucratic structures and mirroring the network structures of their opponents. But this is easier said than done. It can be notoriously difficult for government agencies to genuinely work together and to share intelligence and evidence in joint operations to curb international fraud or disrupt terrorist activities (den Boer et al., 2008). A major policy impetus that emerged from the 9/11 ruins was for the various US security, military, intelligence and police communities to break down the legal and organizational 'walls' that separated them from each other so that they could better share information and personnel (9/11 Commission, 2004: 78–80, 399–428). It is unclear how successful these organizational change efforts have been. And if government bodies themselves work clandestinely in trying to locate and infiltrate shadowy networks, this can raise valid concerns about the overstretch of government power and the bypassing of legal process. When US Vice President Dick Cheney mentioned that government agencies had to work 'through the dark side' in confronting global terror networks that respect no boundaries or principles, critics saw it as a slippery slope that leads through warrantless wiretaps and bulk email interception before arriving at Camp X-Ray and Abu Ghraib (Chwastiak, 2015). Military organizations are keen on network and informational metaphors, with US literature since the 1990s developing a language of 'network-centric warfare', 'power to the edge' and a 'global information grid' (Alberts et al., 2001). Critical scholar James der Derian (2009) brilliantly deconstructs the cultural and organizational ideology of military globalism using his concept of the 'MIME-NET': the military–industrial–media–entertainment-network. His book is a road trip through the mad, violent, cyborg worlds of 'virtual' war.

And yet, like globalization itself, theoretical discussion of the destruction of bureaucracy remains just that – theoretical. Despite the network metaphors, the US Department of Defense remains one of the most bureaucratic and hierarchical organizations imaginable. Large organizations remain addicted to control and top-down authority. Even the extremist terror group ISIS develops rule books, sets up committees and issues monthly financial statements in its efforts to develop its own state among the wreckage of Iraq and Syria (Malik, 2015).

Globalization is widely understood to limit the powers of governments. The internet provides new tools for activists to try to hold governments and corporations to account (Munro, 2015). But the existence of a global information system can also empower formal organizations such as state agencies and law enforcement to *increase* their powers, such as through electronic surveillance of web traffic. In a fascinating document written for the UK government, the barrister David Anderson QC explains why he believes the British government is justified in using 'bulk email interception' (Anderson, 2016). In a world in which private documents can find their way onto the internet and become public for all time, corporate and public organizations are increasingly becoming secretive, keeping looser records, closing the circles of who knows what and covering themselves with opaque, legalistic risk assessment procedures (Costas and Grey, 2016). Democracy, openness and accountability are strangled even as we continue to hear about the virtues of transparency, flexibility and connectivity that the internet age has supposedly given us.

Network structures and the digital information age do exist empirically but, to a large extent, they are also simply the ideological products of globalization. Their growth has occurred alongside the persistence of traditional bureaucracies and hierarchies that remain the centres of corporate and sovereign power. Traditional pyramids are very much still with us. This can be seen clearly when a company or organization gains a new senior leadership team. Often it can be effectively one person – the new CEO, cabinet minister, head teacher or head of department – who comes in wanting to rapidly disrupt everything to 'change the culture' or 'turn the place around'. Power resides at the top and this is immediately made obvious to subordinates as new orders come cascading down.

As with anything related to globalization, the overall picture is paradoxical and confusing. Amid the horizontal networks, value chains, big data, social media, automation, and virtual organizations, it can be hard to determine where the power lies, who is responsible for what actions and inactions and who should be held to account for organizational processes and outcomes. How much power does the top leadership really have in an age of (supposedly) devolved authority? Who is in charge when digital networks and intelligent systems are taking workers further away from the outcomes of their work and replacing human decision-making and discretion?

New ethical dilemmas triggered by global technological and organizational change are perfectly symbolized in the sinister form of the unmanned aerial vehicle, stealthily gliding through the murky skies of the war on terror (Arkin, 2015; Chamayou, 2015). Powers over life and death are invested in algorithms and machines. The drone is an apt metaphor for the latest anxieties about globalization and work – the fears and hopes surrounding automation and the 'rise of the machines'.

Automation and post-work: Global visions of utopia and dystopia

The costs and benefits of replacing working people with machines have been debated since the dawn of industry (Bonneuil and Fressoz,

2013: 258–62). But in a contemporary era dominated by concerns around austerity and precarious work these debates are once again very current. At the time of writing one can barely open a newspaper or click on a media website without coming across bold headlines predicting the further destruction of jobs by the emergence of increasingly competent robots, apps, machine intelligence and the 'internet of things'. We're told that all kinds of job are at risk, not just those in the monotonous and physically exhausting transport, construction or industrial assembly fields, but also well-paid white-collar jobs that involve professional judgement and discretion, such as accounting, actuarial services and medical diagnostics (*BBC News*, 2017; Bregman, 2016; Brynjolfsson and McAfee, 2014; Frey and Osborne, 2017; Suskind and Suskind, 2015). Self-learning 'bots' are even potentially able to work in creative and knowledge work such as journalism and education. Physically capable and increasingly life-like behaviours can be programmed into robots delivering health and social care work. Self-driving cars will eliminate taxi drivers (Ford, 2015).

This literature includes little suggestion that government should try to regulate against the automation of jobs. Automation is portrayed in the same terms as globalization: it is an inevitable process that will affect all our lives and we just have to adapt to it rather than try to stop it or slow it down.

Like offshoring, automation raises a host of ethical, practical and economic dilemmas. Automation can destroy jobs that are poorly paid and unrewarding, but what will happen to those who depended on those jobs? The political Left would usually be expected to defend full employment (which would include low-paid work), but with the prospects for employment for everyone so unlikely, some parts of the Left have started to embrace automation and to encourage the destruction of low-paid work. They argue for a complete rethink of the relationship of work to wages. People whose livelihoods have been destroyed by robots and intelligent systems will be liberated from work but will have to be sustained by radical new government policies such as a universal basic income. The response to automation is usually one of fear, but the rise of artificial intelligence could stimulate us to consider utopian post-work futures, in which automation and universal basic income reduce working hours and boost leisure time (Bregman, 2016; Srnicek and Williams, 2016).

But, as ever, there is room for sceptical interpretations. Doomsday predictions of widespread job loss and the end of work are portrayed as radically new and challenging, but they're not original. They tend to resurface every 20 years or so, particularly in times of economic uncertainty (Granter, 2009). And the much trumpeted 'intelligent' technology is often not as powerful as promoted or feared. Should we really trust a driverless car to reverse-park near a school or put our faith in autopilot systems to land a passenger jet? There are probably good reasons to be sceptical that judges will be replaced by algorithms and prison sentences will be handed down by subroutine. Failures or unexpected outcomes associated with 'intelligent' systems are all-too-common. Automated trading via computer algorithms was partly to blame for the 'flash crash' of 2010 that sent US stock markets plunging in minutes before they largely rebounded in the next half-hour. Some 'issues' took place with 'Tay' – an artificial intelligence 'chatbot' created by Microsoft that was designed to engage in social media conversations with millennials (presumably to jack up internet traffic and hence increase advertising revenues). Within hours of going online it started to send abusive and racist messages, causing some embarrassment to the company. Microsoft quickly withdrew 'Tay' and claimed to be 'making some adjustments' (Wakefield, 2016).

The rhetoric and practice of 'intelligent systems' could be considered yet further symptoms of the 'electronic bullshit' (Crawford, 2009) that surrounds post-industrial work and life. Matthew Crawford, in his celebrated book *Shop Class as Soulcraft* defends the realness and corporeality of craft-based work that has been so badly devalued by the kind of 'global skills training' that privileges a necessarily small 'creative class' of 'symbolic analysts'. Not everyone can be a web-designer, hedge-fund trader or social entrepreneur. We still need people who predominantly work with their hands in the physical realm of making, assisting and repairing: plumbers, hairdressers, builders, care and nursing workers, firefighters, motor mechanics, paramedics, nursing assistants, carpenters. Offshoring and automation may threaten or potentially alter these jobs in interesting ways, but it seems unrealistic to expect the global forces of digitization and automation to destroy them completely.

If one thing is clear from the history of globalization it's that trends can be cyclical and are accompanied by countertrends. While the scale of blue- and white-collar jobs loss due to offshoring was a major political discussion in the early 2000s, about 15 years later we started to see signs of a reversal. America has seen some degree of 're-shoring' of industrial and services work. Moving factories overseas or using offshore contact centres and back-office shared services doesn't always realize as much value as the consultants predict. The need for genuinely high-quality products and customer service has taken the delivery of work back closer to where it is purchased and consumed. Fears over crime, security and intellectual property violations have also played a role, as has the availability of cheaper raw materials via new techniques such as shale gas 'fracking', not to mention the collapse in wages of the workforce left behind by the initial waves of offshoring.

In some sense we see globalization as a victim of its own success – globalization creates its own blowback of de-globalization and reversal (Friedman, 1999: 407). Globalization is variously associated with growing creativity, discretion and knowledge at work, increases in efficiency and productivity, the lowering of costs and the reduction of waste. But it is equally associated with the end of work, employee disaffection, the maintenance of class structures, the abuse of public office and the ruination of corporate and government organization. Dystopian images of globalization in ruins lead us nicely into the final chapter of the book.

6

Globalization – The Fall?

[A]lmost everywhere, we see the possibility of catastrophe.

(Giddens, 1994b: 184)

'*You turn me on. You lift me up, and like the sweetest cup I'd share with you* ...' It is the summer of 1992. The Soviet Union has collapsed and the End of History is blooming. One particular TV commercial is getting a lot of airtime in Britain. Set to the uplifting synth-pop of Simple Minds' *Alive and Kicking*, the advert promotes the transformation of the old English Football League Division One into the new Premier League. Football is being re-imagined as an elite global entertainment franchise – 'a whole new ball game' according to the tagline. The new league is the gilded centrepiece of Rupert Murdoch's Sky TV satellite subscription media empire. But looked at today, this advert doesn't look new at all. In fact, watching in 2017, it looks terribly dated. Traditional gender norms are particularly noticeable: a family man lounges in bed while his wife brings him breakfast; next we see him in the garden of his suburban house making a sprawling save from his son's effort on goal. It has the feel of a Gillette advert, the splashing of water onto a masculine face, the selling of a global brand to consume and celebrate. Professional footballers shower and work out in a gym then jog manfully toward the pitch. Although these sportsmen are clearly well-used to running and gym work, weirdly it all looks stage-managed and unconvincing. In some shots they pose for a giant team photo dressed in their own clubs' real colours. In others they all wear the same confection of a Sky TV football kit. Satellite TV gives us football as franchise: the Premier League is a radical exercise in branding, image-creation and consumerism (Giullianotti, 2002). Football is re-imagined as a million miles from the crumbling terraces, flooded toilets, racist abuse and running battles between rival fans and police that it had become notorious for in the 1970s and 1980s (Back et al., 2001; Goldblatt, 2014). Satellite television has rebooted a tired and failing sport. The shock of Sky TV defibrillated a dying patient. Football is alive (and kicking) again.

This old TV advert provides a fascinating glimpse of how nationally bound the game was back in 1992. It is hard to make out any overseas players, partly because there were so few in the English game at that point. Watching it on a poor quality YouTube video uploaded from what must have been VHS tape, nearly all of them are British or Irish players and most would now be recognizable only to football fans from the era. Personally I can make out the Scottish forward Gordon Strachan, Wimbledon 'hardman' and later action film star Vinnie Jones and the rather less famous John Salako (the latter only because I happen to be a lifelong Crystal Palace supporter). Certain teams are conspicuously present, which is rather poignant given their subsequent decline. Both Sheffield Wednesday and Sheffield United are featured (there is a crass, sanitized nod to their fierce local rivalry), as are – scarcely believable now given their decades of struggle in the lower leagues – Oldham Athletic. Compared to what was to come later, football actually appears quaintly egalitarian; there is no noticeable extra marketing of 'global superbrands' such as Chelsea or Manchester United over and above the other teams featured.

But the ad heralded a new era for English football in which the logics of global capitalism rapidly unfolded (Goldblatt, 2014). The huge influx of cash from the sale of TV broadcast rights around the world led to an explosion of interest that has fundamentally changed the nature of the sport at elite level (Giullianotti, 2002). By 2015 the Premier League sold its TV rights to domestic providers for around £5 billion and to overseas providers for a further £3 billion. Football clubs in the top division are handed more than £100 million in TV money per year, with very little of this trickling down to the lower divisions, or to the amateur, volunteer, grassroots or school levels of the game. Ticket price inflation has priced thousands out of attending matches (Conn, 2005). Players' wages climbed exponentially to the point where today top players are paid around £200,000 per week, and average pros lacking exceptional talent easily make £40,000 per week. Clubs pay transfer fees of £10–15 million just to bring in average footballers. From having none or just one or two overseas players in the starting eleven in the early 1990s (McGovern, 2002), by the mid-2010s English players were on the pitch for only around a third of all the playing time of the top division (Roan, 2014). The English national team failed again and again at international level, possibly because the best English players struggle to play regularly for the top league clubs which are dominated by continental Europeans, South Americans, Africans, or even Koreans and Japanese. By 2014 there were more Argentinian footballers playing in the Premier League than Welsh (Roan, 2014).

Critical voices claim the football world has sold its soul to global satellite broadcasting and advertising. Premier League and Sky TV executives counter by saying that the game has never been more globally successful and they refuse to recognize any narratives of 'greed' or 'corporate sell-out'. Commercially they are right. TV audiences for English football are global and huge screening rights and sponsorship deals can be struck. This indeed brings in huge wealth. But at what cost? Like sports in the USA, everything in the game is now up for sale, such as stadium naming rights (Sandel, 2012). Little is allowed to get in the way of the money-making agenda. Dunkin Donuts recently became the 'official coffee supplier to Liverpool FC'. Yanmar is the industrial tractor partner to Manchester United. Players' wages grow out of all control while clubs can't find the money to adapt stadia to improve wheelchair access, or pay their security, catering, merchandising or maintenance staff anything beyond minimum wage on insecure contracts. Allegations of sharp practice regularly circulate, such as tax evasion, bribery, betting fraud and the use of barely regulated players' agents and middlemen. What used to be an amateur game watched by local working class communities has become a global corporate monster, distorted beyond recognition by liberal flows of cash. Loyal fans feel excluded as football spectators increasingly became customers, tourists or 'football flaneurs' (Guillianotti, 2002).

Football executives flirt with globalizing the game yet further, such as establishing breakaway European leagues featuring only Europe's mega-clubs, or adding an extra game to the English league season played in new overseas 'markets' such as USA, China, UAE and Japan. Premier League chief Richard Scudamore went on record saying he doesn't like the word 'greed' as he doesn't recognize it in the game. He seems to prefer the terminology of management and finance, rhetorically asking: 'When you have monetised the assets, what do you do with it? That's the question' (Holt, 2015).

Controversy has enveloped the game: over ticket prices and rip-off merchandising; over a skewed system that favours the top five or six super-rich clubs who win everything; over the rampant player salary inflation; over tax avoidance and questionable financial practice. Pub owners in England have been convicted for copyright infringement for using continental European satellite receivers to show matches more cheaply than they can on English Sky TV subscriptions. After years of legal battles, the European Court of Justice finally ruled that such convictions are unlawful because Sky's monopolistic control over Premier League broadcasts violates EU laws on a single market for communications services. By working around a loophole, Sky TV continues to issue civil proceedings against those who publicly show Premier League games using overseas transmissions (Spillett, 2015). Sky has also repeated warned it will crack down on illegal internet 'streams' of football matches which are viewed daily in the privacy of peoples' homes.

TV companies try to wrench every last penny out of their 'product' or 'franchise' creating ever-busier schedules that increase the likelihood of player exhaustion or injury and reduce the quality of the play. New tournaments are launched or existing ones expanded which dilutes standards and extends playing seasons so that there is practically no break in the year. Similar issues face all of the world's major sports such as tennis, basketball, athletics, motorsport and cricket (Sage, 2010).

Debates around globalization in sport mirror those around globalization in general. Some celebrate the globalization of sports, suggesting that elite-level sport is becoming more advanced, exciting and virtuous as its internationalization allows it to enhance the lives of ever greater numbers of people. Critics see the globalization of sport as yet another example of the corporatization and monetization processes that delete tradition, subvert community and threaten quality in the pursuit of profit at all costs (Sandel, 2012). Corporate advertisers or overseas owners of sports clubs provoke fan outrage by redesigning badges, moving clubs to different cities, or changing a club's colours or even their names in the quest for more global publicity. For example, the Malaysian owner of Cardiff City FC changed the club's colours from blue to red because red might be regarded as more successful to Asian TV audiences. Globalization doesn't respect notions of tradition or authenticity – such concepts are rooted in a localism that is put on the defensive by the imperatives of market globalism.

As arguably the most globalized of any world sport, football represents the sharpest edges of global capitalism (Veseth, 2010). No wonder we're seeing the rise of critical movements such as #againstmodernfootball which try to defend the local and the traditional. Tribal and identitarian in nature, these movements (often promoted by so-called 'Ultra' fan groups) can veer dangerously close to xenophobia. The logic underlying their angry rejection of the recasting of sport as global enterprise is not far from that of 'jihad globalism' (Steger, 2013) in terms of fans' refusal to compromise on sacred notions of authenticity, localism and tradition and their attempted rejection of a footballing McWorld.

The Simple Minds song from that Premier League advert continues with the line: '*Whatcha gonna do when things go wrong? Whatcha gonna do when it all cracks up?*' This chapter concludes the book by exploring what happens when globalization might go wrong or crack up. Does market globalism generate the dynamics where it might destroy itself? Is global capitalism a victim of its own success? Unable to rein in its greed for more, does globalism, like football, risk devouring itself by destroying the very things that make it unique, valuable and authentic? The same questions hang over other institutions of the post-industrial society, such as universities, art galleries or other cultural industries that might 'sell out' to the logics of global finance and efficiency (see Ritzer, 2007; 2014).

Critical voices from various angles have claimed that the contradictions and excesses of capitalism create the conditions for its own collapse, from Marx who predicted that a disenfranchised global proletariat would overthrow the oppressive capitalist class, to post-structuralists such as Deleuze and Guattari who use psychiatric metaphors of agitation, schizophrenia and delirium to describe the illusory 'progress' of capitalist society (see Noys, 2013: 1–3; Virilio, 2012a: 27). Leftist critics suggest that the contradictions and conflicts over globalization are now so significant that globalization itself is 'in crisis', 'failing' and 'unsustainable' (Freeman and Kagarlitsky, 2004; Perry, 2008; Streeck, 2016). In 2016 – a year of dramatic political turmoil in Europe and America – many observers claimed that we are seeing just these kinds of reversal. The election of Donald Trump as US President and the UK vote to leave the European Union were reported as a turn against globalization and a return to economic nationalism. The profiles of other nationalist, isolationist and xenophobic politicians seemed to be rising, such as Gert Wilders in the Netherlands, or Marine Le Pen in France. Since 2016, it has been common for politicians to describe people from lower socioeconomic backgrounds as those 'left behind' by globalization. *The Wall Street Journal* has warned of the risks of de-globalization (Nixon, 2016). Globalization suddenly seems very unpopular, with media and academic sources describing it as vulnerable or 'in serious trouble' (King, 2017: 5). Thank heavens for Mark Zuckerberg, the founder of Facebook, for coming up with some great ideas to 'reboot' globalization (Ahmed, 2017).

This chapter explores arguments around the possible limits and risks to globalization that might emanate from the very expansion of market globalism – overextensions similar to that experienced by English football as it 'went global'. With frequent economic crises and systemic financial risk, the rejection of cosmopolitan liberalism, the rise of identitarian politics and the ever-present influence of 'justice globalism' challenges to corporate greed, is globalization now in reverse or in decline (Ferguson and Mansbach, 2012: 247–76; Held and McGrew, 2007: xi; King, 2017)? What causes these counter-pressures against the relentless expansion of globalism? Why are they now emanating from both the liberal Left and the conservative Right? The chapter will discuss the ideas of a range of highly pessimistic authors about globalization in chaos, in decline, or heading for a fall. It will explore how *acceleration* lies at the heart of our global condition, and how this constant desire for speed goes hand in hand with discourses of risks and limits. A state of global acceleration and expansion creates feelings of disarray, loss of control and heightened anxiety about crashes and disasters. It creates unpleasant moral challenges in that nothing appears sacred and everything is up for sale.

These concerns are hugely important. But this final chapter also reminds us that risks and fears of calamity and reversal have always been central to globalization discourses (Bauman, 2006; Beck, 2008; Friedman, 1999; Giddens, 1999). Predictions of and desires for de-globalization also have a long history. With this in mind, I argue in this final chapter that while today's pressures for globalization to slow or reverse are currently high, ultimately globalization is not about to imminently reverse or collapse. I suggest that this condition is broadly consistent throughout the diverse domains of globalization; both in globalization literature and in the manifestations of globalism in everyday life. It remains a central issue partly because of the strange phenomenon whereby criticisms, rejections, fears, risks and even scepticism about globalization are wound tightly into the conceptual heart of globalization itself.

Heading for a crash? The dangers of global acceleration

It is common to read that globalization is somehow 'out of control' and heading for disaster. Some of the foundational literature on globalization (for example Giddens, 1991; Held, 1991), while largely positive about increasing global integration, would regularly discuss how increasingly difficult it is for governments, experts and professional bodies to adequately monitor and control globalization. More critical authors portray the entire enterprise of globalization as reckless, as if global elites are pressing ahead with international integration without any real understanding of what they are doing, much less any concern with what ordinary people might think (Greider, 1997). This sense of detachment is an important strand of thinking; conflicts between different groups become more toxic and increasingly irrational as globalization proceeds apace. Globalization in the singular becomes globalizations in the plural. Different visions of globalism pull the world in multiple directions or operate according to different, often clashing, logics (Steger, 2005). According to Virilio (2012a: 27), '[o]ur society has become arrhythmic. Or they only know one rhythm: constant acceleration. Until the crash and systemic failure.' His use of cardiac metaphors hint at emergency, panic and death:

> We are facing the emergence of a real, collective madness rein-
> forced by the synchronization of emotions: the sudden globalization
> of affects in real time that hits all of humanity at the same time,
> and in the name of Progress. *Emergency exit:* we have entered a
> time of general panic. (Virilio, 2012a: 75)

Themes of chaos, breakage and insanity feature heavily in the more
pessimistic literatures on globalization. Coleman (2014) describes the
'lunacy' of contemporary finance theory, suggesting our increasingly
globalized financial system is under-regulated, riven with fraud and
theft and lacks any means for punishing those who have enabled the
reckless risk-taking, unfair accumulation and wanton destruction
associated with the subprime mortgage crisis. Marazzi (2011) describes
financial capitalism as a form of violence. Globalized finance is turbulent, fast paced, unpredictable, like an emergency or a war. Complex
investment models and technologies were supposed to make financial
business remote, computerized, sanitized, logical and risk-free, the
same kind of rhetoric that surrounds contemporary warfighting. One
can think of drone strikes over Syria, Pakistan and Iraq as being governed by the same logics as high-frequency trading: both are forms of
electronically remote gambling dressed up as high-technology progress
(Chamayou, 2015). The risks to the operative are minimal, the effects
on the unsuspecting targets catastrophic. Globalization as war.
Finance as lunacy and violence. New technologies, deregulation and
the rapid integration of societies has unleashed new forces of chaos
and destruction. The runaway train of globalization has hit the buffers. Ordinary people – if they've survived the impact – are left to crawl
from the wreckage without help from the global elites who'd abandoned the controls.

Are there any routes out of this dystopian vision of crises, risk and
reckless acceleration? 'Justice globalism' campaigners call for increased
regulation of global finance, for bankers to be jailed, for tax loopholes
to be closed, for the environment to be better protected, for the drone
strikes to end and military spending to be reined in. But many of these
views fall outside the discussion space in which a supposedly 'global'
corporate news media typically frames what is sensible or even thinka-
ble. Radical suggestions are out of the picture. Mainstream sources
might bemoan the excesses of globalization but will also repeat the
mantra that the broader logics of global free market capitalism are
logical, virtuous and unstoppable. Mainstream media outlets rarely
criticize globalization itself; instead they claim that 'we' had better 'manage' globalization to make it more palatable for people or we face the
likelihood of more Brexits or Le Pens (Friedman, 1999; Stiglitz, 2007).

But political systems around the world are compromised by their deep enmeshment in global capitalism. They are remote from ordinary people, meaning that democratic control and careful reform of global finance are unlikely. Large proportions of the population have lost all faith and trust in the politicians that are supposed to represent them and the professions and experts that are supposed to govern globalization. Many have given up on their prospects improving and are totally disengaged from the political mainstream.

Some academic commentators seem to actively support such a position. Since globalization is 'out of control' let's just sit back and allow global capitalism to go further, deeper, and to observe what happens to societies that get ever more anxious, chaotic and crisis-ravaged. Governments, business leaders and experts will be delegitimized. The system will unravel.

To some extent this view is reminiscent of Marxian ideas about the certainty of proletarian revolution. But Marx's nineteenth century 'scientific' language of the 'laws' of capitalism and the inevitability of revolution is unconvincing and has been repeatedly attacked by other critics of capitalism, such as the countercultural or postmodernist philosophers Deleuze, Guattari, Lyotard and Baudrillard (for an interesting discussion of their doctrines of 'accelerationism' see Noys, 2013). These authors employ similarly excited language to that of other avant-garde cultural critics such as Virilio or Koolhaas in portraying global chaos and general disarray.

More sober analysts, such as Mauro Guillén at the Wharton School of Business, nevertheless also describe an 'architecture of collapse' in which many of the features of the global system (such as international finance, the Eurozone, the awkward relationship of China to the US) are vulnerable to failure and disaster (Guillén, 2015). Certainly these areas are frequently problematic. But when exactly is this 'collapse' coming? We've heard predictions of breakdown and disaster for generations (Bell, 1979). Global capitalism and international political relations are capable of periodic meltdowns but capitalism and human society somehow both persist. While the excited rhetoric of globalism's critics make interesting commentary about globalization, it is not at all clear that it provides realistic prognoses for its actual development. They read more like cultural products of globalization themselves; academic writing as zeitgeist or cultural comment. Acceleration and (episodic) collapse are important features of globalization but they are probably not accurate as signifiers of its whole essence. Financial crises have not led to the collapse of an entire way of life. They have barely put a dent in the doctrines of neoliberalism and market globalism. Banks are bailed out and the status quo ensues.

Having said that, it is important to note that economic crises and inter-connected global financial networks do have important real-world effects such as the destruction of jobs and the stagnation of income (Broughton, 2015; Elliott, 2016). Political conflicts and wars can, of course, be appallingly damaging to individuals and societies (Barber, 1992; Barkawi, 2005; Huntingdon, 1993; Kaldor, 2012). Indeed many political groups (mainstream and fringe) have gained public support by highlighting these effects and linking them directly to abstract, alien, threatening global forces. From Brexit to the 'alt-right' we see claims to slow down, to go back to basics, to isolate and defend ourselves from globalism.

Campaigners for Britain to leave the EU spoke about 'taking back control' and curbing migration. Trump's followers wanted to 'bring the jobs back', 'make America great again' and tear up international trade agreements. This logic could be very significant in that it taps into a broader trope that globalization hasn't crashed or collapsed, or isn't racing away out of control. It's more reflective of a globalization that has already been in retreat for some time, with certain quarters of the Right now as openly critical of globalization as much of the Left has always been. This logic conjures the imagery of globalization facing a long illness and slow deterioration, rather than of spectacular crash and collapse. The following section will explore these interpretations of globalization in decay.

Is globalization already in reverse? Exploring economic stagnation, chaos and isolationism

'Our generation [...] was born in the crisis and has known nothing but economic, financial, social and ecological crisis.' We now exist in 'a world that seems to hold together only through the infinite management of its collapse.' So writes The Invisible Committee (2009: 13–14), a group of Parisian intellectuals behind the radical anarchist text *The Coming Insurrection*. Such writing is emblematic of various pessimistic literatures that suggest globalization has already had its crisis and collapse, that globalization is at the late stage of a long illness. Ecological, financial and security crises are seemingly everywhere. Globalization has a limited lifespan.

> To go on waiting is madness. The catastrophe is not coming, it is here. We are already situated *within* the collapse of a civilization.
> (The Invisible Committee, 2009: 96)

This 'Committee' celebrates and exaggerates globalization's decay and collapse, nostalgically dreaming of revolution and communism.

Other radical writers such as the Italian autonomous Marxist 'Bifo' Berardi (2009) propose a politics of exhaustion, a politics of refusal to engage in global modernity; to go 'off grid', reduce expectations, pursue a slow life (see also Noys, 2013: 94). Maybe such a view is no longer radical. Many mainstream sources believe that the 'advanced' capitalist nations are now locked into a post-growth era. Recession and austerity seem to be with us semi-permanently and everyone except the 1% has given up on seeing a pay rise. BBC News (2017) reported that people in their thirties today have half the wealth that people of the same age had ten years ago.

The UK government launches its 'modern industrial policy' and its 'digital skills strategy', but a disaffected population barely notices. Never-ending economic stagnation, ecological despoliation and chronic budgetary crises have led to the language of 'planned de-growth', or 'living beyond growth'. Elites have started to accept that they have little option but to oversee a managed slowdown of regions with no new jobs and rapidly ageing populations. This is something we've been seeing for some time in some of the world's most economically advanced regions such as Japan, and it's 'coming soon to a city near you' (Matanle and Sato, 2010).

The global security situation remains another intractable problem. There is no end in sight to the global war on terror or 'long war' against extremism. Like the 'war on drugs' the war on terror is by its nature open-ended and lacks a victory scenario. Instead, the influence of global terror networks, like global warming or systemic global financial risk, is a 'wicked problem' that cannot be solved. It's just something we'll have to learn to live with. Governments, law enforcement and emergency services develop strategies of 'resilience' and 'preparedness', essentially accepting that violence and panic are almost inevitable. Anti-terror training exercises see armed police swarming through shopping centres in Brussels or rescuing hostages on the Thames. Abandoned industrial facilities are re-designated as 'mass casualty clearing centres'. The infinite management of collapse. For their part, terror groups claim that their attacks are responses to the state-sponsored terrorism of Western nations that they also see as entrenched and never-ending.

Andrew Hill (2008) writes of the 'spectacularity' of terrorism and counter-terrorism. 24/7 global news media somehow intermeshes terrorism with other elements of everyday life, magnifying its impact to remote audiences. On the evening of Friday 13 November 2015, global terrorism met international football. A multiple 'marauding firearms incident' terrorized the city of Paris, including a suicide bomb attack at the Stade de France, where the French national football team was playing Germany. ISIS claimed the attacks were a response to French airstrikes on ISIS positions in Syria and Iraq. Just four days later the France team played a match against England in London. Wembley stadium was lit up with the French tricolore, and *La Marseillaise* rang out before kick-off. *Liberté, égalité, fraternité* were emblazoned in an electronic light show across the stadium walls. Some described being moved to tears by the sense of solidarity between two nations that shared in the 'global' vision of freedom, democracy, peace and the Enlightenment. Global mega-events of terrorism and sport seemed to bring countries together in tragedy.

But again we're reminded of the unpredictable (il)logics of globalization and de-globalization. Just three months after this show of European solidarity, Britain had voted to leave the EU altogether. New barriers between people go up just as others are coming down. Early in his presidency, Donald Trump tried to ban entry to the USA by travellers from certain majority-Muslim nations. With chaos at American airports and visa requirements tightened in many countries, Ohmae's (1991) 'borderless world' thesis now looks completely wrong. A nasty counter-global image is conjured by Trump's planned 'great, beautiful wall' to seal the United States' border with Mexico. Unmanned drones will patrol it. Close your eyes and you can visualize Trump's wall and hear the distant buzzing of electronic surveillance systems. 'There. You hear it. The humming' (Kobek, 2011: 10).

In some important senses the world has *de-globalized* in recent decades. Fears over migration and terrorism have encouraged governments and citizens to look inward and reject integration. Political and cultural relations between certain nations remain frosty and seem to be worsening, such as that between the USA and Iran. Some of these relationships were actually closer during the Cold War. In 1956, the US State Department organized a cultural diplomacy mission designed to portray the US as culturally sophisticated, open, and non-racist. The 'Jazz Ambassadors' project involved many of America's top jazz musicians playing a very successful tour of Iran. Jazz icons such as Dizzy Gillespie played to packed houses. The current climate of the war on terror makes it difficult to imagine such events today, suggesting that political and cultural globalization has gone into reverse.

There seems to be no logic to it. Globalization simultaneously creates integration and division at different times and places. The violence of cults such as ISIS or of state-sponsored counter-terror operations appear almost equally random and nihilistic (Chamayou, 2015). Badiou (2016) claims that the rise of identitarian politics around ethnicity, sexuality, gender and nationhood means we have given up conceptualizing our shared identity as humans. Pankaj Mishra's *The Age of Anger*

(2017) nicely encapsulates the deep irrationality and self-destructive divisions of contemporary 'global' society.

But others will dispute such a pessimistic view and will deny that these conflicts mean that globalization is in reverse. The world is not going to hell propelled by irrational hatreds and fears. Taking a longer historical view some argue that global violence is actually in progressive decline (Pinker, 2011). Civility, peace, respect for the person, and intercultural integration are a reality in more parts of the world now than at any other time in history. A global consciousness can arguably exist in some form, and certain notions of universal human rights and international solidarity can be made tractable. In the 1930s the sociologist Norbert Elias wrote of the 'civilizing process' by which ideas of good, healthy, respectable, and appropriate behaviours came to be increasingly encoded and established by states and by civil society (see Pinker, 2011: 71–97). Michel Foucault opens his classic work *Discipline and Punish* (1979: 3–6) with a thoroughly revolting description of the torture and dismemberment of a man who tried to murder King Louis XV of France in 1757. Executions were carried out under the auspices of church and state and conducted as public spectacle. Foucault discusses how and why such an event would be unthinkable in almost all societies of today where punishment has developed into an essentially private and (comparatively) humane process. There are few reasons to believe that modernization and globalization are making people more barbaric, more violent and less integrated than in earlier historical epochs which saw widespread incivility and chaos, colonial empires, total wars, genocide and religious crusades (Pinker, 2011; Kaldor, 2012: 15–31). The continued existence of intercultural violence today does not mean that globalization has failed, collapsed or eroded.

Even amid the New Wars (Kaldor, 2012) of the post-1990s globalization era we still see the existence of globalization as an active force. Tarak Barkawi, in *Globalization and War* (2005: 169), argues that:

> [...] war can be seen as an occasion for interconnection, as a form of circulation between combatant parties. In and through war, societies are transformed, while at the same time societies shape the nature of war. War is reconfigured as a globalizing force, as a multidimensional form of connection and constitution between people and places.

Warring parties – like cultures, ethnicities or identities in general – are not singular, immutable, sealed-off units but complex, multi-faceted social constructs. Recent years have seen the growing privatization of war and the confusing interspersal of non-state actors into various warzones, such as overseas volunteers, irregulars, mercenaries and members of terror or crime networks (Kaldor, 2012). War and the military play a far greater role in constituting globalization that has been commonly recognized in the globalization literature.

Military strategist Carl von Clausewitz in 1832 famously described war as 'the continuation of politics by other means'. Globalization might be thought of as the continuation of capitalism by other means. Issues of technology, politics, nation, regulation, trade and identity never seem to recede and have always been central points of debate since the advent of industrial capitalism. There is an annoying sense of 'presentism' in the globalization literature, a lack of historical sensitivity (see Osterhammel and Petersson, 2005; and Chapter 2 of the present volume). This weak thinking is exemplified by Fukuyama's (1992) infamous declaration that post-Cold War market globalism marks 'the end of history'. Excited globalization rhetoric continues to give the impression of a radically new age (Anthony, 2017) when in reality almost every element of present-day globalization can be related in some form to enduring elements of human existence, especially since the rise of international capitalism since the late nineteenth century.

If this is true for globalization, it is also true for today's counter-globalist trends and the repeated declarations of globalization in ruins. We've heard of globalization's crises before: after the 1999 Seattle riots, after 9/11, after Lehman Brothers (Ferguson and Mansbach, 2012: 247–90). Street protests against transnational governance organizations such as the WTO and IMF – highly reminiscent of the Seattle and Genoa protests of the late 1990s – recur in locales less often reported on, such as the protests in Manila at the Apec trade summit in 2015. The 1%, Occupy and Uncut movements have kept alter-globalization on the news agenda in the West at least to some degree. There is little reason to think that the current counter-global trends mark the reversal or end of globalization.

Reflecting on Chapter 2 above, it is helpful to think of globalization as primarily a rhetorical device. Brexit can just as easily be portrayed as in keeping with globalization rather than evidence of global decline. British politicians were overwhelmingly against leaving the EU, but when the referendum unexpectedly gave a 'Leave' result of 52%, the fence-sitting MPs immediately switched to promoting Brexit and 'a Global Britain' that will perform well on the international stage once freed of European ties. New slogans were developed of 'Britain is Great' and 'Exporting is Great'. The 'global' tag seems never to go out of fashion, even when it is highly tangential or basically meaningless. Perhaps its meaninglessness is precisely what makes this concept so fashionable.

Like other management buzzwords like 'innovation', 'leadership' or 'flexibility', it can be made to mean anything their users want.

The tangled paths of Brexit (and the related referendum on Scottish independence from Britain) remind us that regional, national, and pan-national identities are fluid and contested, sometimes fragile and unstable. Recent electoral and rhetorical rejections of EU or global identities suggest that these often struggle to carry much weight (Badiou, 2016). Globalization theorist Tony Giddens had written about all this in some depth in the early 1990s (Giddens, 1991) and identity politics has always been a key part of globalization literature. Wars and insurgencies magnify the importance of identity and geographic place amid the supposedly de-localized arenas of markets, ideology or ethnicity (Kaldor, 2012). When the ISIS group seized the city of Dabiq it made great play of this in its media output. This victory was supposedly prophesized (Withnall, 2016). But, interestingly, no-one in the West seemed to have heard of the place. Among 24/7 news and a global consciousness, we shouldn't forget humanity's potential for living in parallel, incommensurate worlds. A great example was a tragicomic gaffe by US Presidential candidate Gary Johnson during the campaign trail in 2016. 'What is Aleppo?' he asked, apparently totally unaware of one of the worst humanitarian disasters of recent decades. He was widely ridiculed. But in a strange way he unwittingly made a very important statement about how ignorant the supposedly 'global' world is of humanity's diverse histories, geographies, cultures and identities. 'Global news media' is anything but global; it is often hermetically sealed and inward-looking. If they were being honest, many people in the Western world would also not have heard of Aleppo if not for the reporting of the war in Syria. And until some event deemed 'newsworthy' is broadcast by Fox News, the BBC or Russia Today, they will likely remain ignorant of dozens of other locations of varying cultural, mythic, economic or religious importance, just as millions of people in Asia or the Middle East probably haven't heard of Stonehenge or Philadelphia.

The 'global' claims of any person or organization will only ever be partial. ISIS claims to be a global pan-Islamic movement. Johnson and his followers believe that their zero-state libertarianism is a global, rational force for progress, liberty and wealth generation. But they all delude themselves if they are arrogant enough to think they are the arbiters of rationality, truth and justice, and that the world will flock to their cause. Rather, such views are the result of what Columbia University's Mark Lilla memorably calls *The Shipwrecked Mind* (Lilla, 2016), an irrational, largely emotional response to change and disruption leading to feelings of being unwanted, marginalized and rendered objectionable by a new mainstream. Again, as Lilla and Mishra (among others) clearly show, none of these developments is new. The presentism of globalization theory (and of much media commentary) shrouds the fact that capitalism and modernity has always created those who fear catastrophe, feel marginalized and remain nostalgic for safer, more just and more 'authentic' times past. Capitalism has always united and divided people simultaneously in these and other ways, as this final section will try to show.

Conclusion – 'Globalization' as a new word for 'capitalism'

We're now right at the tail end of this supposedly 'very short' ramble through the vast, fragmented libraries of globalization. In what remains I will attempt to come to some sort of a conclusion, even as the scope of debate makes this an impossibility.

What I have tried to show in this book is that globalization is in one sense radically new but in another simply a continuation of fundamental trends of human existence. Periodically (such as the current time of writing) we often hear of it reaching its limits, collapsing or reversing. But globalization has always progressed unevenly. While expanding in some geographic, economic, technological and social areas, it falls back in others. It has always contained inherent conflicts and limitations. Free trade encourages wealth generation and technological innovation, but free competition and open borders also exposes people, firms and governments to uncertainty and poverty.

The globalization literature thus continually features counter-global trends: nationalism and isolationism, borders and migration, tariffs and regulation. While progressive 'civil society' advocates discuss the need for more cosmopolitan outlooks as a way to promote globalism, justice and peace (Beck, 2000; Giddens, 1994a; Held et al., 1999; Kaldor, 2012), the prospects for this outlook to really flower across the majority of the world's population don't look especially encouraging (Martell, 2007). Even if a cosmopolitan, progressive, post-traditional globalism does develop and spread further, it is doubtful that we will ever shake off the feeling that globalization does actually damage large swathes of the world's population, no matter what the cosmopolitan experts say (see Chapter 3).

Cosmopolitans will argue that locals are small-minded and unwilling to see the bigger picture of how globalization equates to a more progressive, just and wealthy world. But a cosmopolitan world-view is often in tension with the other roots from which people's identities and values are derived. The question concerns to what and whom we are most comfortable relating. These elements are often mostly local in their direct impact – see the enduring power of the themes of family, God or war as referred to in that Google Ngram graphic from Chapter 1. Many will accept the idea that 'the local and the global intermingle' (Steger, 2013: 15), but the most powerful wellsprings of identity and personhood often seem more likely to surround local, traditional, or even tribal formations (Ghemawat, 2011: 321). The global marketplace will always threaten to 'sell out' the authentic and the local, but there is always the risk that local blowback will be so severe that the globalists have to back off. Cardiff City's club colours eventually went back to blue. If globalization creates such feelings of insecurity and artificiality, and if the global elites seem increasingly remote and their worldviews so inauthentic, then it is perhaps no mystery why localism can be so resurgent and globalism so unpopular. If the President of the United States professes anti-cosmopolitan and anti-globalist sentiments then many will take this as evidence of globalization in retreat. When Donald Trump or his supporters call someone a 'globalist' they mean it as a grave insult. He is the first major world leader since the Second World War to openly promote tariffs and protectionism as a central part of his economic policy.

But declarations of the fall of globalization are almost certainly premature. Even President Trump has powerful historical echoes. In his rhetoric of 'America First', and in building a giant border wall, he repeats the immigration panics and Red Scare of the 1920s that targeted Italian or Irish migrants as communists, anarchists and criminals who will undercut wages and generally sow destruction. As Richard Hofstadter (1964) wrote a year after the Kennedy assassination, there is nothing new about the 'paranoid style' in American politics. In *Come Home, America,* William Grieder, a long-time commentator on US politics and globalization, discussed a sense in which American government, society and economy was failing ordinary people:

> People don't claim to know all the economic facts and theories, but they can see what's happening around them. The lost jobs, the closed factories, the middle-aged men working behind the counter at Starbucks. [...] Most Americans are not opposed to the idea of global trade, and they accept the inevitability of globalization. What they are against is the unaddressed consequences globalization will have for their country. [...] Opinion leaders overwhelmingly regard new trade agreements as good for the country. Less than half of the public agrees. (Grieder, 2005: 70)

That was 2005. One wonders why Trump's electoral success seemed so shocking when the fear of job loss and the resentment of ordinary people towards elites and experts had been well-documented for over ten years (Klein, 2017). Much more could be done by these elites to convince ordinary people that globalization and free trade really are progressive forces. But they won't have success in this aim by just *telling* people this. They need to *show* it, by helping to put in place structures that actually do serve to improve peoples' lives. This is much harder to do as it will require large-scale investment in jobs, skills, schools, healthcare, infrastructure, law enforcement, government: all things that the profit incentive often threatens.

In an article published in the first issue of *Globalizations* journal, Professor of Global Politics Barry Gills ventures that 'in truth, the world is indeed one family' (Gills, 2004: 3). In the closing pages of *Beyond Left and Right*, Anthony Giddens (1994a: 253) speculates about 'universal values' such as 'the sanctity of human life' and 'an obligation to promote cosmopolitan solidarity'. Many of us might want to agree with such sentiments. It is often hard to see them reflected in reality, but we can perhaps live in hope. One heartening story was kind of a re-run of the 'Jazz Ambassadors' visit to Iran. In 2015 American jazz composer Bob Belden took his band on a hugely successful tour of Iran, selling-out opera houses and meeting 'just pure love' (Reich, 2015). In a way, this second trip was an improvement on the first, in that it wasn't a government-run, stage-managed event. It appears to have been much more spontaneous and authentic. Belden recalls:

> [d]ay to day, Islam is no different than any other religion in the world: It comes down to what you do with it and how you express it. And we saw the same exact human condition and situations that you would see anywhere else in the modernized world. (Quoted in Reich, 2015)

People the world over tend to want essentially the same basic things. Relations between sworn enemies can thaw. Events, actions and artefacts (especially creative, artistic or musical) can remind us of our shared humanity. The grubby incentives of global commerce can sow the seeds of division but can also help to promote peace between trading nations (Pinker, 2011). From 1942–5 Japan and America were engaged in one of the most brutal conflicts of modern history, but by the mid-1980s elements of cultural integration had been leveraged by the commercial imperatives of a global capitalism (Kelts, 2006). The simple urge to make a living and to trade with others can create new forms of integration. Even resistance to globalization is enabled by and, in some sense, contributes to a global consciousness. Naomi Klein advocates:

> [...] a citizen-centered alternative to the international rule of the brands. That demand, still sometimes in some areas of the world whispered for fear of a jinx – is to build a resistance – both high-tech and grassroots, both focused and fragmented – that is as global, and as capable of coordinated action, as the multinational corporations it seeks to subvert. (Klein, 2010: 446)

Critical and mainstream globalization literature often focuses on the power and influence of giant multinational firms. But 'low-level' globalization goes on in cities and towns around the world. The connections to other regions through migration, the search for work, or for sanctuary from war and persecution, and the technological systems that enable these connections are almost inescapable. Stroll down a less upscale street in a major British city and you'll see shops selling phone cards for cheap calls to Nigeria, Brazilian-owned evangelical churches, Polish cafés. Shopfronts will tell stories of a distinctly low-end globalization, but a globalization that is surely real: 'Glory Investments', 'Shiraz Palace', 'The Mixed Blessings Bakery', 'Wall of Sound Pentecostal Ministries', 'Wok This Way', 'Big Mama Jerk Centre'. Globalization is visibly enmeshed into everyday life in the most mundane ways and is surely likely to remain a powerful theme of life despite the repeated discussions of stagnation, isolation, crisis and collapse (Ray, 2007).

Such discussions take us back to the debates of Chapter 2 and those sceptical writers who suggest that globalization is too broad a concept to be precise. I can certainly accept that view. Yet this imperfect term 'globalization' does capture something important and remains powerfully relevant. Many discuss globalization as a process or an end result. I prefer to think of globalization simply as a *theme*. Like other themes (good and evil, love, betrayal, comradeship, vengeance) it reflects a very broad element of the human existence than many of us can relate to. Rather than the decline and fall of globalization, the political reversals of 2016 have put the theme of globalization very much back on the media agenda. This is why I think the reports of globalization's death are greatly exaggerated.

Having said that, there is one area that I have only hinted at in this book that does have the potential to radically scale back globalization. The risks associated with environmental despoliation and climate change are a major feature of the globalization literature (Giddens, 1994a, 2011; Held and McGrew, 2007: 64–72; Steger, 2013: 87–102) and are a huge area of concern for the world's population. Noam Chomsky (2012: 84) argues that 'we are coming close to the edge of a precipice of environmental destruction'. Some describe the Anthropocene – a geological epoch triggered by human activity that has changed the world's physical and biological nature, perhaps fundamentally and irreversibly (Bonneuil and Fressoz, 2013). Global industrial capitalism runs the risk of ultimately destroying itself by making the planet unfit for organic life. James Lovelock's famous 'Gaia' thesis envisages the entire world as one giant living ecosystem, with humankind's position on it highly ambivalent: 'in some ways the human species is like a planetary disease, but through civilization we redeem ourselves and have become a precious asset for the Earth' (Lovelock, 2007: 13). We live in hope that global capitalism is civilized enough to permit and encourage the technological creativity and genuine international cooperation that is requited to deal with this global problem.

These hopes and fears recall the opening of this book where I discuss the rise of a 'global' environmental consciousness. Images of a vulnerable 'spaceship Earth' emerged in the 1960s. People, governments and corporations often tend to ignore such truly 'global' concerns as environmental catastrophe because the immediate concerns of the local and the here-and-now are more visible and urgent. Despite the ubiquity of the globalization theme, we often fail to identify with the global and privilege the local in our everyday lives (Ghemawat, 2011). Planet Earth is everyone's home but the imperatives and routines of our own homes and local communities often dominate our consciousness and behaviours.

This is not necessarily to condemn the local, or to criticize it as small-minded and parochial. The sociologist Les Back recently wrote an astute article about how local community rituals and prominent local individuals, can play central roles in making life liveable among the vicissitudes of unemployment, austerity and social change that are all somehow bound up in this thing we call 'globalization'. He argues that 'people refuse to be crushed by those destructive forces' (Back, 2015: 832) as he describes one particular family which makes an annual effort to decorate its house with the most colourful Christmas lights show imaginable. One resident, named Alex, says: 'I think it's people who have never had nothin' who like to give back to people' (Back, 2015: 831).

I began this book with a story about Christmas. It seems appropriate to end the book the same way as it gives us a sense of completion. But one thing seems certain – the debates without end surrounding the nature, impact and realities of globalization won't ever be wrapped up quite so neatly.

References

9/11 Commission (2004) *Final Report of the National Commission on Terrorist Attacks Upon the United States*. New York: W.W. Norton.

Acker, J. (2004) 'Gender, capitalism and globalization', *Critical Sociology*, 30(1): 17–41.

Adler, W.M. (2000) *Mollie's Job: A Story of Life and Work on the Global Assembly Line*. New York: Scribner.

Adorno, T. and Horkheimer, M. (1987/2002) *Dialectic of Enlightenment: Philosophical Fragments*. Redwood City, CA: Stanford University Press.

Ahmed, K. (2017) 'Zuckerberg: My Facebook manifesto to re-boot globalisation', *BBC News*, 16 February.

Alberts, D.S., Gartska, J.J., Hayes, R.E. and Signori, D.A. (2001) *Understanding Information Age Warfare*. Washington, DC: Command and Control Research Programme.

Albrow, M. (1996) *The Global Age: State and Society Beyond Modernity*, Cambridge: Polity.

Amin, A. (1994) 'Post-Fordism: Models, fantasies and phantoms of transition', in A. Amin (ed.), *Post-Fordism: A Reader*. Oxford: Blackwell, pp. 1–39.

Anderson, D. (2016) *Report of the Bulk Powers Review*. London: HMSO.

Anderson, M. (2015) 'World Bank data shows number of "low-income" countries halved since 1994', *The Guardian*, 10 July.

Ang, I. (1985) *Watching Dallas: Soap Opera and the Melodramatic Imagination*. London: Methuen

Anthony, A. (2017) 'Homo sapiens will change into something different …', *The Observer*, 19 March.

Appelbaum, R.P. and Robinson, W.I. (2005) 'Introduction: Toward a critical globalization studies – continued debates, new directions, neglected topics', in R.P. Appelbaum and W.I. Robinson (eds), *Critical Globalization Studies*. Abingdon: Routledge, pp. xi–xxxiii.

Arkin, W.M. (2015) *Unmanned: Drones, Data, and the Illusion of Perfect Warfare*. New York: Little, Brown.

Back, L. (2015) 'Why everyday life matters: Class, community and making life livable', *Sociology*, 49(5): 820–36.

Back, L., Crabbe, I. and Solomos, J. (2001) *The Changing Face of Football: Racism, Identity and Multiculture in the English Game*. Oxford: Berg.

Badiou, A. (2016) *Our Wound is not so Recent: Thinking the Paris Killings of 13 November*. Cambridge: Polity.

Barber, B.R. (1992) 'Jihad vs. McWorld', *The Atlantic Monthly*, 269(3): 56–63.

Barber, B.R. (2011) *Jihad vs. McWorld: Terrorism's Challenge to Democracy*. London: Corgi.

Barkawi, T. (2005) *Globalization and War*. Lanham, MD: Rowman & Littlefield.

Barley, S.R. and Kunda, G. (2006) *Gurus, Hired Guns and Warm Bodies: Itinerant Experts in a Knowledge Economy*. Princeton: Princeton University Press.

Bauman, Z. (1998) *Globalization: The Human Consequences*. Cambridge: Polity.

Bauman, Z. (2000) *Liquid Modernity*. Cambridge: Polity.

Bauman, Z. (2006) *Liquid Fear*. Cambridge: Polity.

BBC News (2000) 'Fears for DiCaprio's Beach', 10 February.

BBC News (2017) 'Robots to affect up to 30% of jobs, says PwC', 24 March.

Beck, U. (1992) *Risk Society: Towards a New Modernity*. London: Sage.

Beck, U. (1999) *World Risk Society*. Cambridge: Polity.

Beck, U. (2000) *What is Globalization?* Cambridge: Polity.

Beck, U. (2008) *World at Risk*. Cambridge: Polity.

Bell, D. (1976) *The Coming of Postindustrial Society: A Venture in Social Forecasting*. New York: Basic Books.

Bell, D. (1979) *The Cultural Contradictions of Capitalism*. London: Heinemann.

Berardi, F. (2009) *The Soul at Work: From Alienation to Autonomy*. Cambridge, MA: Semiotext(e).

Bhagwati, J. (2007) *In Defense of Globalization*. Oxford: Oxford University Press.

Birnbaum, R. (2000) 'The life-cycle of academic management fads', *The Journal of Higher Education*, 71(1): 1–16.

Blair, T. (2001) *Speech to the Labour Party Conference*, 2 October.

Blinder, A. (2006) 'Offshoring: The next industrial revolution?', *Foreign Affairs*, 85(2): 113–28.

Bluestone, B. and Harrison, B. (1982) *The Deindustrialization of America: Plant Closings, Community Abandonment, and the Dismantling of Basic Industry*. New York: Basic Books.

Bonneuil, C. and Fressoz, J.-B. (2013) *The Shock of the Anthropocene: The Earth, History and Us*. London: Verso.

Bozkurt, Ö. (2015) 'The punctuation of mundane jobs with extreme work: Christmas at the supermarket deli counter', *Organization*, 22(4): 476–92.

Branson, R. (2014) *The Virgin Way: How to Listen, Learn, Laugh and Lead*. London: Virgin Books.

Brech, E., Thompson, A. and Wilson, J.F. (2010) *Lyndall Urwick: Management Pioneer*. Oxford: Oxford University Press.

Bregman, R. (2016) *Utopia for Realists*. Amsterdam: De Correspondent.

Broughton, C. (2015) *Boom, Bust, Exodus: The Rust Belt, the Maquilas, and a Tale of Two Cities*. Oxford: Oxford University Press.

Brown, G. (2016) 'Leaders must make the case for globalisation', *Financial Times*, 17 July.

Bryman, A. (1999) 'The Disneyization of society', *The Sociological Review*, 47(1): 25–47.

Brynjolfsson, E. and McAfee, A. (2014) *The Second Machine Age: Work, Progress and Prosperity in a Time of Brilliant Technologies*. New York: W.W. Norton.

Burawoy, M., Blum, J.A., George, S., Gille, Z. and Thayer, M. (2000) *Global Ethnography: Forces, Connections and Imaginations in a Postmodern World*. Oakland, CA: University of California Press.

Cahill, T. (2015) '10 taxpayer handouts to the super rich that will make your blood boil', *US Uncut*, 28 October.

Cairncross, F. (2001) *The Death of Distance: How the Communications Revolution is Changing Our Lives*. Harvard, MA: Business School Press.

Carmody, P. (2011) *The New Scramble for Africa*. Cambridge: Polity.

Castells, M. (2000) *The Rise of the Network Society*, 2nd edn. Oxford: Blackwell.

Centino, M.A. and Cohen, J.N. (2010) *Global Capitalism: A Sociological Perspective*. Cambridge: Polity.

Chakrabortty, A. (2015) 'The £93bn handshake: Business pocket huge subsidies and tax breaks', *The Guardian*, 7 July.

Chamayou, G. (2015) *Drone Theory*. London: Penguin.

Chang, H.J. (2003) *Kicking Away the Ladder: Development Strategy in Historical Perspective*. London: Anthem.

Chomsky, N. (2002) *Media Control: The Spectacular Achievements of Propaganda*. New York: Seven Stories Press.

Chomsky, N. (2012) *Occupy*. London: Penguin.

Chomsky, N. (2013) *On Anarchism*. London: Penguin.

Chwastiak, M. (2015) 'Torture as normal work: The Bush administration, the Central Intelligence Agency and "enhanced interrogation techniques"', *Organization*, 22(4): 493–511.

Cohen, R. (2007) 'Creolization and cultural globalization: The soft sounds of fugitive power', *Globalizations*, 4(3): 369–84.

Cole, T. (2012) 'The white-savior industrial complex', *The Atlantic*, 21 March.

Coleman, L. (2014) *The Lunacy of Modern Finance Theory*. Abingdon: Routledge.

Conn, D. (2005) *The Beautiful Game: Searching for the Soul of Football*. London: Yellow Jersey.

Cooke, W. (2003) 'The denial of slavery in management studies', *Journal of Management Studies*, 40(8): 1895–918.

Cornwell, R. (2011) '9/11 lost decade: The American dream and the missing years', *The Independent*, 10 September.

Costas, J. and Grey, C. (2016) *Secrecy at Work: The Hidden Architecture of Organizational Life*. Redwood City, CA: Stanford University Press.

Crawford, M.B. (2009) *Shop Class as Soulcraft: An Inquiry into the Value of Work*. New York: Penguin.

de Botton, A. (2009) *The Pleasures and Sorrows of Work*. London: Hamish Hamilton.

den Boer, M., Hillebrand, C. and Nölke, A. (2008) 'Legitimacy under pressure: The European web of counter-terrorism networks', *Journal of Common Market Studies*, 46(1): 101–24.

der Derian, J. (2009) *Virtuous War: Mapping the Military-Industrial-Media-Entertainment-Network*. Abingdon: Routledge.

Devereaux, R. (2012) 'Video goes viral, and so do concerns about its producers', *The Guardian*, 7 March.

Dicken, P. (2007) *Global Shift: Mapping the Changing Contours of the World Economy*. London: Sage.

Dore, R. (2000) *Stock Market Capitalism: Welfare Capitalism: Japan and Germany versus the Anglo-Saxons*. Cambridge: Cambridge University Press.

Doremus, P.N., Keller, W.W., Pauly, L.W. and Reich, S. (1999) *The Myth of the Global Corporation*. Princeton: Princeton University Press.

Easton, M. (2014) 'Is Britain really becoming more racist?' *BBC News*, 28 May.

Eatwell, R., and Goodwin, M.J. (2010) 'Introducing the 'new' extremism in twenty-first century Britain', in Eatwell, R., and Goodwin, M.J. (eds.) *The New Extremism in 21st Century Britain*. Abingdon: Routledge, pp. 1–20.

Egan-Wyer, C., Muir, S.L., Pfeiffer, A. and Svensson, P. (2014) 'The ethics of the brand', *ephemera*, 14(1): 1–11.

Elliott, L. (2016) 'Up to 70% of people in developed countries "have seen incomes stagnate"', *The Guardian*, 14 July.

Ellis, B.E. (1991) *American Psycho*. London: Picador.

Ellsberg, D. (2004) *Secrets: A Memoir of Vietnam and the Pentagon Papers*. London: Penguin.

Feldman, S.P. (2013) *Trouble in the Middle: American–Chinese Business Relations, Culture, Conflict and Ethics*. Abingdon: Routledge.

Ferguson, J. (2006) *Global Shadows: Africa in the Neoliberal World.* Durham: Duke University Press.

Ferguson, Y.H. and Mansbach, R.W. (2012) *Globalization: The Return of Borders to a Borderless World?* Abingdon: Routledge.

Fichtner, J. (2014) 'Privateers of the Caribbean', *Competition & Change*, 18(1): 37–53.

Florida, R. (2012) *The Rise of the Creative Class, Revisited.* New York: Basic Books.

Food and Agriculture Organization of the United Nations (2015) *The State of Food Insecurity in the World: Meeting the 2015 International Hunger Targets: Taking Stock of Uneven Progress.* Rome: FAO.

Ford, M. (2015) *The Rise of the Robots: Technology and the Threat of Mass Unemployment.* London: Oneworld Publications.

Foucault, M. (1979) *Discipline and Punish: The Birth of the Prison.* London: Peregrine.

Frank, T. (2001) *One Market Under God: Extreme Capitalism, Market Populism, and the End of Economic Democracy.* New York: Martin Secker and Warburg.

Frayne, D. (2015) *The Refusal of Work: The Theory and Practice of Resistance to Work.* London: Zed Books.

Freeman, A. and Kagarlitsky, B. (2004) 'Introduction: World Empire – or a World of Empires?' in A. Freeman and B. Kagarlitsky (eds), *The Politics of Empire: Globalisation in Crisis.* London: Pluto, pp. 1–45.

Frey, C.B. and Osborne, M.A. (2017) 'The future of employment: How susceptible are jobs to computerisation?', *Technological Forecasting and Social Change*, 114(1): 254–80.

Friedman, T. (1999) *The Lexus and the Olive Tree.* London: HarperCollins.

Friedman, T. (2007) *The World is Flat: The Globalized World in the Twenty-First Century.* London: Penguin.

Fukuyama, F. (1992) *The End of History and the Last Man.* New York: Free Press.

Furedi, F. (2006) *The Culture of Fear Revisited.* London: Continuum.

Ghemawat, P. (2009) 'Why the world isn't flat', *Foreign Policy*, 159: 54–60.

Ghemawat, P. (2011) *World 3.0: Global Prosperity and How to Achieve It.* Cambridge, MA: Harvard Business School Press.

Giddens, A. (1991) *The Consequences of Modernity.* Cambridge: Polity.

Giddens, A. (1994a) *Beyond Left and Right: The Future of Radical Politics.* Cambridge: Polity.

Giddens, A. (1994b) 'Risk, trust, reflexivity', in U. Beck, A. Giddens and S. Lash, *Reflexive Modernization.* Cambridge: Polity, pp. 184–215.

Giddens, A. (1999) *Runaway World: How Globalisation is Reshaping our Lives.* London: Profile.

Giddens, A. (2011) *The Politics of Climate Change*. Cambridge: Polity.

Gilens, M., and Page, B.I. (2014) 'Testing theories of American politics: Elites, interest groups, and average citizens', *Perspectives in Politics*, 12(3): 564–81.

Gill, A.A. (2005) *AA Gill is Away*. London: Simon & Shuster.

Gills, B.K. (2004) 'The turning of the tide', *Globalizations*, 1(1): 1–6.

Giullianotti, R. (2002) 'Supporters, followers, fans, and flaneurs: A taxonomy of spectator identities in football', *Journal of Sport and Social Issues*, 26(1): 25–46.

Glasgow University Media Group (1976) *Bad News*. London: Routledge and Kegan Paul.

Glennie, J. (2008) *The Trouble with Aid: Why Less Could Mean More for Africa*. London: Zed Books.

Goldblatt, D. (2014) *The Game of Our Lives: The Meaning and Making of English Football*. London: Penguin.

Golding, T. (2002) *The City: Inside the Great Expectation Machine*. London: FT Prentice Hall.

Gottfried, H. (2004) 'Gendering globalization discourses', *Critical Sociology*, 30(1): 9–15.

Graeber, D.R. (2013) 'On the phenomenon of bullshit jobs', *Strike!*, August 17.

Granter, E. (2009) *Critical Social Theory and the End of Work*. Farnham: Ashgate.

Granter, E. (2017) 'Strictly business: Critical Theory and the society of rackets', *Competition & Change*, 21(2): 94–113.

Gregg, M. (2011) *Work's Intimacy*. Cambridge: Polity.

Greider, W. (1997) *One World, Ready or Not: The Manic Logic of Global Capitalism*. London: Penguin.

Greider, W. (2005) *Come Home, America: The Rise and Fall (and Redeeming Promise) of our Country*. New York: Rodale.

Guillén, M. (2001) 'Is globalization civilizing, destructive, or feeble? A critique of five key debates in the social science literature', *Annual Review of Sociology*, 27: 235–60.

Guillén, M. (2015) *Architecture of Collapse: The Global System in the 21st Century*. Oxford: Oxford University Press.

Hancock, P. and Rehn, A. (2011) 'Organizing Christmas', *Organization*, 18(6): 737–45.

Hannerz, U. (1990) 'Cosmopolitans and locals in world culture', *Theory, Culture & Society*, 7(2): 237–51.

Hansen, V. (2012) *The Silk Road: A New History*. Oxford: Oxford University Press.

Harding, C. (2016) 'How Japan came to believe in depression', *BBC News*, 20 July.

Hardt, M. and Negri, A. (2000) *Empire*. Cambridge, MA: Harvard University Press.

Hartman, A. (2015) *A War for the Soul of America: A History of the Culture Wars*. Chicago: University of Chicago Press.

Hassard, J., McCann, L. and Morris, J. (2009) *Managing in the Modern Corporation: The Intensification of Managerial Work in USA, UK and Japan*. Cambridge: Cambridge University Press.

Hay, C. and Marsh, D. (2000) 'Introduction: Demystifying Globalization', in Hay, C. and Marsh, D. (eds.), *Demystifying Globalization*. Basingstoke: Macmillan, pp. 1–17.

Hayes, R.H. and Abernathy, W.J. (1980) 'Managing our way to economic decline', *Harvard Business Review*, July–August: 67–77.

Heath, J. and Potter, A. (2006) *The Rebel Sell: How the Counterculture became Consumer Culture*. Chichester: Capstone.

Held, D. (1991) 'Democracy and the global system', in D. Held (ed.), *Political Theory Today*. Cambridge: Polity, pp. 1–21.

Held, D. and McGrew, A. (2007) *Globalization/Anti-Globalization: Beyond the Great Divide*. Cambridge: Polity.

Held, D., McGrew, A., Goldblatt, D. and Perraton, J. (1999) *Global Transformations*. Cambridge: Polity.

Hill, A. (2008) *Re-imagining the War on Terror: Seeing, Waiting, Travelling*. Basingstoke: Palgrave.

Hirst, P., and Thompson, G. (2001) *Globalization in Question*, 2nd edn. Cambridge: Polity.

Hirst, P., Thompson, G. and Bromley, S. (2009) *Globalization in Question*, 3rd edn. Cambridge: Polity.

Ho, K. (2009) *Liquidated: An Ethnography of Wall Street*. Durham, NC: Duke University Press.

Hofstadter, R. (1964) 'The paranoid style in American politics', *Harper's*, November: 77–86.

Hofstede, G. (2003) *Culture's Consequences: Comparing Values, Behaviors, Institutions and Organizations across Nations*. London: Sage.

Holt, O. (2015) 'Premier League boss Richard Scudamore defends his multi-billion pound success story: "I don't like the word "greed" ... I don't know what it means"', *Daily Mail*, 8 August.

Holton, R.J. (2012) *Global Finance*. Abingdon: Routledge.

Hopper, P. (2007) *Understanding Cultural Globalization*. Cambridge: Polity.

Huntingdon, S. (1993) 'The clash of civilizations?' *Foreign Affairs*, Summer: 22–49.

Ignatieff, M. (1994) *Blood & Belonging*. London: Vintage.

Irvine, C. (2013) 'Kremlin returns to typewriters to avoid computer leaks', *The Daily Telegraph*, 11 July.

Jackson, D. (2016) 'Donald Trump targets globalization and free trade as job killers', *USA Today*, 28 June.

Jalan, R. (1997) 'An Asian Orientalism? Libas and the textures of post-colonialism', in A. Scott (ed.), *The Limits of Globalization*. London: Routledge, pp. 90–115.

James, P. and Steger, M.B. (2014) 'A genealogy of "globalization": The career of a concept', *Globalizations*, 11(4): 417–34.

Jay, M. (1992) *Marxism and Totality: The Adventures of a Concept from Lukacs to Habermas*. Berkeley: University of California Press.

Jenkins, R. (2012) *Being Danish: Paradoxes of Identity in Everyday Life*. Copenhagen: Museum Tusculanum Press.

Jessop, B. (2000) 'The crisis of the national spatio-temporal fix and the ecological dominance of globalizing capitalism', *International Journal of Urban and Regional Studies*, 24(2): 323–60.

Johnson, C. (2002) *Blowback: The Costs and Consequences of American Empire*. London: Little, Brown.

Johnson, C. (2006) *The Sorrows of Empire: Military, Secrecy and the End of the Republic*. London: Verso.

Kaldor, M. (2012) *New and Old Wars: Organized Violence in a Global Era*. Cambridge: Polity.

Kaldor, M. (2015) 'Five meanings of global civil society', in M. Steger (ed.), *The Global Studies Reader*. Oxford: Oxford University Press.

Kaplan, R.D. (1993) *Balkan Ghosts: A Journey through History*. New York: Random House.

Kapur, A., Macleod, N. and Singh, N. (2005) 'Plutonomy: Buying luxury, explaining global imbalances', *Citigroup Global Markets*. Available at: www.slate.com/blogs/moneybox/2011/11/21/the_economics_of_plutonomy.html (accessed 30 November 2016).

Keane, J. (2003) *Global Civil Society*. Cambridge: Cambridge University Press.

Kelts, R. (2006) *Japanamerica: How Japanese Pop Culture Has Invaded the US*. Basingstoke: Palgrave Macmillan.

Klein, N. (2007) *The Shock Doctrine*. London: Penguin.

Klein, N. (2010) *No Logo*. London: Fourth Estate.

Klein, N. (2017) *No is not Enough: Defeating the New Shock Politics*. London: Allen Lane.

Klikauer, T. (2013) *Managerialism: A Critique of an Ideology*. Basingstoke: Palgrave.

King, S.D. (2017) *Grave New World: The End of Globalization, the Return of History*. New Haven, CT: Yale University Press.

Kiss, J. (2015) 'Welcome to Jun, the town that ditched bureaucracy to run on Twitter', *The Guardian*, 2 July.

Kobek, J. (2011) *ATTA*. Cambridge, MA: Semiotext(e).

Kobek, J. (2016) *I Hate the Internet: A Novel*. London: Serpent's Tail.

Kochhar, R. (2015a) 'A global middle class is more promise than reality', *Pew Research Center*, 8 July.

Kochhar, R. (2015b) 'Seven-in-ten people globally live on $10 or less per day', *Pew Research Center*, September 23.

Koolhaas, R. (2002) 'Junkspace', *October*, 100: 175–90.

Kumar, K. (2007) 'Global civil society', *European Journal of Sociology*, 48(3): 413–34.

Lash, S. and Lury, C. (2007) *Global Culture Industry: The Mediation of Things*. Cambridge: Polity.

Latour, B. (2004) 'Why has critique run out of steam? From matters of fact to matters of concern', *Critical Inquiry*, 30: 225–48.

Leach, W. (1993) *Land of Desire: Merchants, Power, and the Rise of a New American Culture*. New York: Vintage.

Lessig, L. (2008) *Remix: Making Art and Commerce Thrive in the Hybrid Economy*. London: Penguin.

Lilla, M. (2016) *The Shipwrecked Mind: On Political Reaction*. New York: The New York Review of Books.

Lindahl, H. (2013) *Fault Lines of Globalization: Legal Order and the Politics of A-Legality*. Oxford: Oxford University Press.

Lockard, C.B. and Wolf, M. (2012) 'Occupational employment projections to 2020', *Monthly Labor Review*, January: 84–108.

Lovelock, J. (2007) *The Revenge of Gaia*. London: Penguin.

Maddison, A. (2007) *Contours of the World Economy, 1–2030 AD*. Oxford: Oxford University Press.

Malik, S. (2015) 'The Isis papers: Behind "death cult" image lies a methodical bureaucracy', *The Guardian*, 7 December.

Marazzi, C. (2011) *The Violence of Financial Capitalism*. Cambridge, MA: Semiotext(e).

Marlowe, L. (2014) 'Luxleaks: Former PwC employee admits he took files', *The Irish Independent*, 15 December.

Martell, L. (2007) 'The third wave in globalization theory', *International Studies Review*, 9: 173–96.

Martell, L. (2010) *The Sociology of Globalization*. Cambridge: Polity.

Matanle, P. and Sato, Y. (2010) 'Coming soon to a city near you! Learning to live "beyond growth" in Japan's shrinking regions', *Social Science Japan Journal*, 13(2): 187–210.

Maxton, G.P. and Wormald, J. (2004) *Time for a Model Change: Re-engineering the Global Automotive Industry*. Cambridge: Cambridge University Press.

McCann, L. (2014a) *International and Comparative Business: Foundations of Political Economies*. London: Sage.

McCann, L. (2014b) 'Disconnected amid the networks and flows: Employee detachment from company and union after offshoring', *British Journal of Industrial Relations*, 52(2): 237–60.

McCann, L. (2016) 'From management to leadership', in S. Edgell, E. Granter and H. Gottfried (eds), *The Sage Handbook of Sociology of Work and Employment*. London: Sage, pp. 167–84.

McGovern, P. (2002) 'Globalization or internationalization? Foreign footballers in the English League, 1946–95', *Sociology*, 36(1): 23–42.

McNeil, W.H. (2015) 'Globalization: Long-term process of new era in human affairs?', in M.B. Steger (ed.), *The Global Studies Reader*. Oxford: Oxford University Press.

Metcalfe, D. (2009) *Out of Steppe: The Lost Peoples of Central Asia*. London: Arrow.

Milanovic, B. (2016) *Global Inequality: A New Approach for the Age of Globalization*. Cambridge, MA: Belknap Press of Harvard University Press.

Milkman, R. (1991) *Japan's California Factories: Labor Relations and Economic Globalization*. Los Angeles, CA: University of California, Los Angeles Institute of Industrial Relations.

Mills, C.W. (1956/2000) *The Power Elite*. Oxford: Oxford University Press.

Mishra, P. (2016) 'Welcome to the age of anger', *The Guardian*, 8 December.

Mishra, P. (2017) *The Age of Anger: A History of the Present*. London: Allen Lane.

Mittelman, J.H. (2000) *The Globalization Syndrome: Transformation and Resistance*. Princeton: Princeton University Press.

Mittelman, J.H. (2004) 'Globalization debates: Bringing in microencounters', *Globalizations*, 1(1): 24–37.

Morrison, A. and Rabellotti, R. (2009) 'Knowledge and information networks in an Italian wine cluster', *European Planning Studies*, 17(7): 983–1006.

Moses, K. (2013) 'China leads the waste recycling league', *The Guardian*, 14 June.

Munck, R. (2002) 'Global civil society: Myths and prospects', *International Journal of Voluntary and Nonprofit Organizations*, 13(4): 349–61.

Munro, I. (2015) 'Organizational resistance as a vector of deterritorialization: The case of WikiLeaks and secrecy havens', *Organization*, 23(4): 567–87.

NASA (2014) *Apollo 8: Christmas at the Moon*. Available at: https://www.nasa.gov/topics/history/features/apollo_8.html.

Naughton, B. (2007) *The Chinese Economy: Transitions and Growth*. Cambridge, MA: MIT Press.

Nederveen Pieterse, J. (1995) 'Globalization as hybridization', in M. Featherstone, S. Lash and R. Robertson (eds), *Global Modernities*. London: Sage.

Nederveen Pieterse, J. (2009) *Globalization and Culture: Global Mélange*. New York: Rowman & Littlefield.

Nixon, S. (2016) 'Risk of deglobalization hangs over world economy', *Wall Street Journal*, 16 October.

Nordstrom, C. (2004) *Shadows of War: Violence, Power, and International Profiteering in the Twenty-First Century*. Berkeley: University of California Press.

Nordstrom, C. (2007) *Global Outlaws: Crime, Money and Power in the Contemporary World*. Berkeley: University of California Press.

Norris, P. and Inglehart, R. (2009) *Cosmopolitan Communications: Cultural Diversity in a Globalized World*. Cambridge: Cambridge University Press.

Noys, B. (2013) *Malign Velocities: Accelerationism and Capitalism*. Winchester: Zero.

Nye, J.S. (2005) *Soft Power: The Means to Success in World Politics*. New York: PublicAffairs.

Obermeyer, Z., Murray, C.J.L. and Gakidou, E. (2008) 'Fifty years of violent war deaths from Vietnam to Bosnia: Analysis of data from the world health survey programme', *British Medical Journal*, 336: 1482–6.

Ohmae, K. (1991) *The Borderless World: Power and Strategy in the Interlinked Economy*. London: Fontana HarperCollins.

Osterhammel, J. and Petersson, N.P. (2005) *Globalization: A Short History*. Princeton: Princeton University Press.

Park, G.-S., Jang, Y.S. and Lee, H.Y. (2007) 'The interplay between globalness and localness: Korea's globalization revisited', *International Journal of Comparative Sociology*, 48(4): 337–53.

Parker, M. (2008) 'Memories of the Space Race: From Apollo to cyberspace', *Information, Communication & Society*, 11(6): 846–60.

Parreñas, R.S. (2001) *Servants of Globalization: Women, Migration, and Domestic Work*. Redwood City, CA: Stanford University Press.

Patterson, R. and Huff, S.M. (1999) 'The decline and fall of Esperanto: Lessons for standards committees', *Journal of the American Medical Informatics Association*, 6(6): 444–6.

Pauly, L.W. and Reich, S. (1997) 'National structures and multinational corporate behavior: Enduring differences in the age of globalization', *International Organization*, 51(1): 1–30.

Pedhazur, A. and Perliger, A. (2006) 'Introduction: Characteristics of suicide attacks', in A. Pedazhur, (ed.), *Root Cause of Suicide Terrorism: The Globalization of Martyrdom*. Abingdon: Routledge, pp. 1–12.

Perrucci, R. and Perrucci, C. (2008) *America at Risk: The Crisis of Hope, Trust, and Caring*. Lanham, MD: Rowman and Littlefield.

Perry, A. (2008) *Falling off the Edge: Globalization, World Peace, and Other Lies*. London: Pan.

Peters, T. (1992) 'Introduction', in D.M. Armstrong, *Managing by Storying Around: A New Method of Leadership*. New York: Currency, pp. xv–xvii.

Peters, T. (2001) 'Tom Peters' True Confessions', *Fast Company*, 21 December, 53: 78–92.

Pickerill, J. and Krinsky, J. (2015) 'Why does Occupy matter?', in J. Pickerill, J. Krinsky, G. Hayes, K. Gillan and B. Doherty (eds), *Occupy! A Global Movement*. Abingdon: Routledge, pp. 1–9.

Piketty, T. (2014) *Capital in the Twenty-First Century*. Cambridge, MA: Belknap Press of Harvard University Press.

Piketty, T., Saez, E. and Zucman, G. (2016) *Distributional National Accounts: Methods and Estimates for the United States*, National Bureau of Economic Research Working Paper 22045. Cambridge, MA: National Bureau of Economic Research.

Pilger, J. (2016) *The New Rulers of the World*. London: Verso.

Pinker, S. (2011) *The Better Angels of Our Nature*. London: Penguin.

Raab, M., Ruland, M., Schönberger, B., Blossfeld, H.-P., Hofäcker, D. and Buchholz, S. (2008) 'GlobalIndex: A Sociological Approach to Globalization Measurement', *International Sociology*, 23(4): 596–631.

Rabellotti, R. and Schmitz, H. (1999) 'The internal heterogeneity of industrial districts in Italy, Brazil and Mexico', *Regional Studies*, 33(2): 97–108.

Rainnie, A., Barrett, R., Burgess, J. and Connell, J. (2008) 'Introduction: Call centres, the networked economy and the value chain', *Journal of Industrial Relations*, 50(2): 195–208.

Ray, L. (2007) *Globalization and Everyday Life*. Abingdon: Routledge.

Reich, H. (2015) 'Jazz diplomacy: An American in Tehran', *Chicago Tribune*, 17 March.

Reich, R.B. (1991) *The Work of Nations: Preparing Ourselves for 21st Century Capitalism*. London: Simon & Shuster.

Reinert, E.S. (2007) *How Rich Countries Got Rich … and Why Poor Countries Stay Poor*. London: Constable.

Reiser, O.L. and Davies, B. (1944) *Planetary Democracy: An Introduction to Scientific Humanism*. New York: Creative Age.

Reuben, A. (2016) 'Zero-hours contracts rise to 903,000 workers', *BBC News*, 8 September.

Ritzer, G. (2007) *The Globalization of Nothing 2*. Thousand Oaks: Sage.

Ritzer, G. (2010) *Globalization: A Basic Text*. Chichester: Wiley-Blackwell.

Ritzer, G. (2014) *The McDonaldization of Society*, 8th edn. London: Sage.

Roan, D. (2014) 'Are foreign players really damaging the Premier League?' *BBC News*, 20 November.

Roberts, J. (2005) 'The Ritzerization of knowledge', *Critical Perspectives on International Business*, 1(1): 56–63.

Robertson, R. (1992) *Globalization: Social Theory and Global Culture*. London: Sage.

Robertson, R. (1994) 'Globalisation or glocalisation?' *The Journal of International Communication*, 1(1): 33–52.

Robins, N. (2006) *The Corporation that Changed the World: How the East India Company Shaped the Modern Multinational*. London: Pluto.

Rosenberg, J. (2000) *The Follies of Globalisation Theory: Polemical Essays*. London: Verso.

Ryoo, W. (2009) 'Globalization, or the logic of cultural hybridization: The case of the Korea wave', *Asian Journal of Communication*, 19(2): 137–51.

Sadowski, Y. (1998) *The Myth of Global Chaos*. Washington, DC: Brookings Institution Press.

Sage, G.H. (2010) *Globalizing Sport: How Organizations, Corporations, Media, and Politics are Changing Sports*. Abingdon: Routledge.

Sandel, M. (2012) *What Money Can't Buy: The Moral Limits of Markets*. London: Allen Lane.

Sassen, S. (2006) *Cities in a Global Economy*. London: Sage.

Scholte, J.A. (2005) *Globalization: A Critical Introduction*. Basingstoke: Palgrave.

Sheppard, E. (2016) *Limits to Globalization: Disruptive Geographies of Capitalist Development*. Oxford: Oxford University Press.

Sklair, L. (2000) *The Transnational Capitalist Class*. Oxford: John Wiley and Sons.

Spillett, R. (2015) 'Pub landlord wins eight-year battle to overturn conviction for showing Premier League matches on foreign channels instead of paying for Sky', *Daily Mail*, 1 April.

Srnicek, N. and Williams, A. (2016) *Inventing the Future: Postcapitalism and a World Without Work*. London: Verso.

Steger, M.B. (2005) *Globalism: Market Ideology Meets Terrorism*. Lanham, MD: Rowman & Littlefield.

Steger, M.B. (2006) *The Rise of the Global Imaginary: Political Ideologies from the French Revolution to the Global War on Terror*. Oxford: Oxford University Press.

Steger, M.B. (2013) *Globalization: A Very Short Introduction*. Oxford: Oxford University Press.

Steger, M.B. and Roy, R.K. (2010) *Neoliberalism: A Very Short Introduction*. Oxford: Oxford University Press.

Stiglitz, J.E. (2002) *Globalization and its Discontents*. London: Penguin.

Stiglitz, J.E. (2007) *Making Globalization Work*. London: Penguin.

Stiglitz, J.E. (2013) *The Price of Inequality*. London: Penguin.

Stiglitz, J.E. and Bilmes, L. (2008) *The Three Trillion Dollar War: The True Cost of the Iraq Conflict*. London: Allen Lane.

Strange, S. (1996) *The Retreat of the State: The Diffusion of Power in the World Economy*. Cambridge: Cambridge University Press.

Streeck, W. (2016) *How Will Capitalism End? Essays on a Failing System*. London: Verso.

Sturgeon, T.J. (2002) 'Modular productions networks: A new American model of industrial organization', *Industrial and Corporate Change*, 11(3): 451–96.

Susskind, R. and Susskind, D. (2015) *The Future of the Professions: How Technology will Transform the Work of Human Experts*. Oxford: Oxford University Press.

Sutcliffe, B. and Glyn, A. (1999) 'Still underwhelmed: Indicators of globalization and their misinterpretation', *Review of Radical Political Economics*, 31(1): 111–31.

Taylor, A. (2001) *American Colonies: The Settling of North America*. London: Penguin.

Taylor, P. and Bain, P. (2005) '"India calling to the far away towns": The call centre labour process and globalization', *Work, Employment and Society*, 19 (2): 261–82.

Taylor, W.C. and Webber, A.M. (1996) *Going Global: Four Entrepreneurs Map the New World Marketplace*. London: Penguin.

The Invisible Committee (2009) *The Coming Insurrection*. Cambridge, MA: Semiotext(e).

Thompson, G. (2014) *Globalization Revisited*. Abingdon: Routledge.

Thorne, K. (2005) 'Designing virtual organizations? Themes and trends in political and organizational discourses', *Journal of Management Development*, 24(7): 580–607.

Turkle, S. (2011) *Alone Together: Why We Expect More from Technology and Less From Each Other*. New York: Basic Books.

Urwick, L.F. (1974) 'V.A. Graicunas and the span of control', *The Academy of Management Journal*, 17(2): 349–54.

Veseth, M. (1998) *Selling Globalization: The Myth of the Global Economy*. Boulder, CO: Lynne Rienner.

Veseth, M. (2010) *Globaloney 2.0: Unravelling the Myths of Globalization*. Lanham, MD: Rowman and Littlefield.

Vine, D. (2015) *Base Nation: How US Military Bases Abroad Harm America and the World*. New York: Metropolitan Books.

Virilio, P. (2012a) *The Administration of Fear*. Cambridge, MA: Semiotext(e).

Virilio, P. (2012b) *The Great Accelerator*. Cambridge: Polity.

Wakefield, J. (2016) 'Microsoft chatbot is taught to swear on Twitter', *BBC News*, 24 March.

Wallerstein, I. (2004) *World-Systems Analysis: An Introduction*. Durham, NC: Duke University Press.

Wang, G. and Yeh, E.Y. (2005) 'Globalization and hybridization in cultural products: The cases of *Mulan* and *Crouching Tiger, Hidden Dragon*', *International Journal of Cultural Studies*, 8(2): 175–93.

Waring, S.P. (1991) *Taylorism Transformed: Scientific Management Theory since 1945*. Chapel Hill: University of North Carolina Press.

Weiss, L. (1998) *The Myth of the Powerless State: Governing the Economy in a Global Era*. Ithaca: Cornell University Press.

Westwood, R.I. and Jack, G. (2007) 'Manifesto for a post-colonial international business and management studies: A provocation', *Critical Perspectives on International Business*, 3(3): 246–65.

Withnall, A. (2016) 'Isis loses "prophesied" town of Dabiq to Syrian rebels after a short battle', *The Independent*, 16 October.

Wolf, M. (2004) *Why Globalization Works*. New Haven, CT: Yale University Press.

Wolf, M. (2006) 'Forces for globalization win the day', *Financial Times*, 12 September.

Wright, L. (2006) *The Looming Tower: Al-Qaeda's Road to 9/11*. London: Penguin.

Yano, C.R. (2011) 'Reach out and touch someone: Thinking through Sanrio's social communication empire', *Japanese Studies*, 31(1): 23–36.

Index